IT HURTS TO WIN

THE OFFICIAL INSIDE STORY OF THE 2022-23
STANLEY CUP® CHAMPION VEGAS GOLDEN KNIGHTS®

SKYBOX PRESS

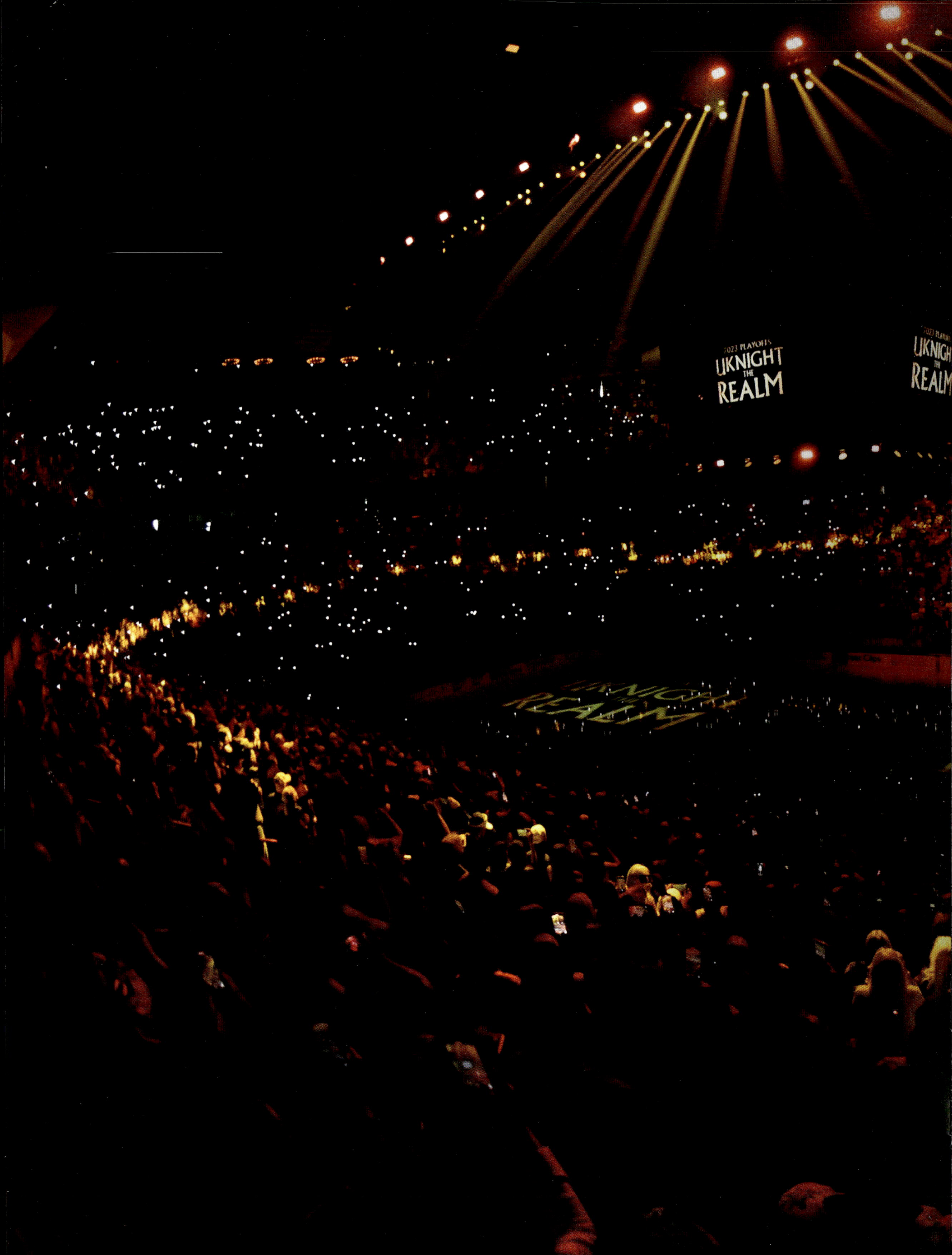
2023 PLAYOFFS
UKNIGHT
THE
REALM

CUP
IN SIX
BY BILL FOLEY

Much has been made about my prediction that our expansion franchise would win the Stanley Cup in six years, especially since that glorious night June 13 when it came true.

At the time, the quote sparked some scoffs around the National Hockey League: "Who is this guy? Doesn't he know how hard it is to win in this league?"

In some places – think about Canada – the reactions were even harsher: "When he can only sell tickets to tourists, isn't the better question where he'll relocate the team in six years?"

After our inaugural-season success, it didn't seem that outlandish. But by the fall of 2022, entering year six, we were trying to rebound after missing the playoffs.

As I reflect on the "Cup in six" comment now, it wasn't exactly a prediction or a deadline. What it really represented was a standard of excellence that I wanted to set, not just in year six but from the start. We wanted to be bold, we wanted to be ambitious, and we didn't want to settle for the typical arc of an expansion franchise. I have always set what many believe are unrealistic goals and aspirations because the intent of the organizations I'm involved with is one of always exceeding expectations and, in the eyes of many, overachieving. I don't believe we overachieved; we simply always advanced, never retreated, and we never, never, never gave in, nor did we give up.

From the very beginning, I have been proud of the way we have risen to what many saw as an unrealistic result.

At first it was just a small group of staff members. George McPhee assembled a hockey operations department that was not only talented but also boasted high character. We strived to do things right, and, if we missed that mark, to make it right.

Soon we had a group of players – the Misfits – who exceeded expectations, in part because our own standard was set so high. No one was content with missing the playoffs just because expansion teams were supposed to; we were motivated – not just by outside doubters but also by a collective drive to succeed.

Along the way we saw the Las Vegas community embrace the Golden Knights in a truly meaningful way. Some of that was borne from the tragedy of October 1, which we will never forget. I was proud of the way our team responded then, again exceeding most people's expectations for a group of professional athletes, most of whom were new to the city. It also came from an overall sense of civic pride that found an outlet on the ice and in The Fortress.

I knew when we started the initial season ticket drive that this community was hungry for a team like the Golden Knights to call its own. I went into that effort with high expectations, but even I might have underestimated the support here.

That support only fueled our desire to keep getting better. We wanted to Always Advance, and each year I felt we were building to something. We made big-time additions like Mark Stone, Alex Pietrangelo, and Jack Eichel. But we also made shrewd under-the-radar moves, like trades for Chandler Stephenson, Nicolas Roy, and Adin Hill.

By 2022–23, we had assembled a perfect combination of talent, determination, and togetherness that could not be topped. The season that this book chronicles wasn't easy, but we saw our group rise up to meet every challenge. The ability to do that starts with setting high expectations.

Whenever I can, I try to join our players for lunch or breakfast in their lounge at City National Arena.

Last season, every day the players entered that room, they passed a large replica of the Stanley Cup. It's not a picture, or a painting – it's an actual cup, fittingly gold, bearing the words "THE QUEST."

So sure, "Cup in six" was bold and maybe brash. But, most important, it was ambitious, and it was defined. It was more than a quote – it was something the organization could see, in 3D, daily.

It was then pursued by a group of people who thrived when the bar was set that high.

That's why there's no need to make predictions for years seven, eight, or beyond. The standard has been set.

Thanks to the team featured in these pages for making it a reality.

A CHARACTER WIN

BY GEORGE MCPHEE

Bill Foley was awarded an NHL franchise for Las Vegas on June 22, 2016. I immediately sent my résumé to Bill, and he called a week later. Our 45-minute conversation did not go as expected. I thought the applicant was to sell himself to the owner. Instead, Bill Foley was the salesman selling the applicant on the opportunity in Las Vegas.

Within a week, we had a deal, and a very defined understanding and goal of delivering the Stanley Cup to Vegas.

Over the next 60 days, 35 talented but low-ego people were hired in Hockey Operations. One of the earliest was the incomparable Kelly McCrimmon. A few months into our Vegas Golden Knights careers, when Kelly and I had a better grasp of the Vegas community, our owner, fan support, facilities, and lifestyle, we had, like many of the decisions we've made, the same thought at the same time. We expressed, "If we do our jobs here, we can win" – meaning, we can win it all: the Stanley Cup.

Now, as we enjoy the reality of winning the Stanley Cup, it is easy to forget what a bold goal that was. After all, many NHL teams have never won a Stanley Cup, and many others have won a Cup but haven't done so for several decades. Winning the Cup is hard. The Golden Knights won a Stanley Cup in our sixth season! Not to mention reaching the Final in our first season, and four conference finals in six seasons.

In 2016 – a full year before we knew which players might be available to us – we started by defining what we wanted in our players. Also, we wanted our culture to be a difference maker.

The skating, talent, and intelligence that comprise so much of traditional hockey evaluation were part of what we wanted, but we knew that could only take us so far. Every team is on the lookout for those attributes, and, heading into an expansion draft, we knew the other 30 teams would be protecting those players.

To reach the heights we aspired to, we identified character, leadership, and competitiveness as qualities that would define the players we wanted. As we got to know Bill, it was not surprising that these attributes and our culture – what we thought would help elevate the team's performance – fit seamlessly with his West Point background.

"Always Advance" was more than a motto on our office walls. Everything we did was defined by our desire to win, and we wanted to find players with that same drive. We were exceptionally well organized for the expansion draft, and our strategy delivered players with the values we coveted.

Our blueprint and culture certainly contributed to our unprecedented success in the first season. As we continued to build our team, we never lost sight of what we valued in players. Outsiders said we chased every "shiny toy" available, but many

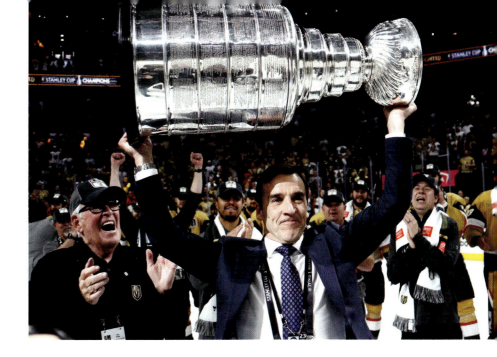

knowledgeable hockey people realized we were aggressively advancing and building a formidable team. If you watched our team in the spring of 2023, you saw how players like Mark Stone, Alex Pietrangelo, and Jack Eichel personified leadership, character, and compete. In those cases and many others, we had done our homework – we knew what we were getting in both the player and the person. Our foundation of players already embodied leadership, character, and compete, and each addition to our team made us and our culture stronger.

As the celebrations from the Stanley Cup reverberate, the importance of those qualities are even more clear. We all know why we won. With our new coach, Bruce Cassidy, we could see it and feel it in the spirit of our team as the players progressed through training camp. It was even more evident in the way they bonded during the season, and overcame challenges like the injuries to our goalies and our captain.

When we hit the All-Star break and knew Stone would miss at least the rest of the season – and might never play again – we were nervous about a repeat of the year before, when injuries had sent us into a death spiral. Fortunately, the break allowed us to stabilize, reset, and prepare to advance down the stretch. You could see the power of our culture in a team of leaders in our locker room beyond the captain.

Once the playoffs arrived, we were a team that was all business, and whose character and togetherness helped mitigate any pressure to win. The group's bond was so authentic that when faced with challenges, the players looked forward to tackling them. Nothing bothered these players.

We were dominant for big stretches in the playoffs, particularly in elimination games, when it can be so tough to beat a team a fourth time. And we never faced elimination ourselves, which might be the best testament to just how good our team was. The group did a great job of staying in the moment and not looking ahead, which is a cliché, but it's a fact, and you know it when you see it.

Beyond the locker room, the community's support helped create that powerful environment as well. Could you imagine a more energizing place to play than T-Mobile Arena? Part of that traced back to the connection our team made with the Las Vegas Valley in the first season. In the face of the October 1 tragedy, our players recognized they were in a situation that was about more than hockey. What every one of those high-character players did to help people grieve, heal, and prosper was remarkable. Our culture, strength, and connection with our community remains with this team and organization to this day.

That community support around the Stanley Cup win – from the festive atmosphere of Game 5 to the parade day and beyond – has helped make this all feel real. In many ways, when you are handed the Stanley Cup for the first time, you don't feel worthy. That was my initial thought as Kelly handed it to me: 'Did we really do this?'

As I reflect on this journey, and the way this community has embraced our team, the reality sinks in. As confident as we were about what our team and organization were capable of, it's still hard to believe that the Vegas Golden Knights won the Stanley Cup.

The words and photos in this book are one more step in making it all feel real. And still that wonderful feeling of awe remains – and always will.

BUILDING A
CHAMPION
BY KELLY MCCRIMMON

Six weeks later, after hosting our family's day with the Stanley Cup, it still seems surreal that we are the Stanley Cup champions. While I am not a person who spends much time reminiscing, I can only view this incredible accomplishment first from a macro perspective before dialing in on the championship season that was 2022-23.

So many things immediately come to mind. I had worked 27 successful seasons with the Brandon Wheat Kings of the Western Hockey League as an owner, general manager and head coach before getting a call from George McPhee in late July 2016. George had recently been hired as general manager of the expansion NHL team in Las Vegas, and we had never met. Anyone in the hockey industry would immediately be taken aback by how uncommon this is. It is practically a given that people hire those with whom they have worked in the past or have a previous affiliation. Little did I know that this man would become a great mentor, a trusted friend, and a person for whom I would have tremendous respect and admiration. Furthermore, neither of us would have ever imagined that seven years later, we would be Stanley Cup champions.

Any conversation about the success of our team begins with the 2016–17 season, prior to expansion – one of the most fascinating years of my career

and of every person who took part. The work we did, the hiring of an amazing staff, the strategy, the negotiating, the deal making, and the deep-dive analysis of all 30 NHL teams – it was like earning your NHL undergraduate degree and master's degree, all in 11 months.

As many things as we did correctly predict, we did not anticipate the success our franchise achieved in that inaugural 2017–18 season. After collecting 109 points in the regular season, followed by playoff wins over the rival Los Angeles Kings and San Jose Sharks, and then defeating a very talented Winnipeg Jets team, we advanced to the Stanley Cup Final. This was an unprecedented accomplishment by an expansion team in any sport.

It was a team of castoffs, later known by the moniker the Misfits – which still holds true to this day and can be found on the championship rings of Will Carrier, William Karlsson, Brayden McNabb, Reilly

Smith, Shea Theodore, and Conn Smythe winner Jonathan Marchessault. This team was selfless – there was no hierarchy, no entitlement. They all had something to prove, and there was complete buy-in to Gerard Gallant and his coaching staff. The combination of these attributes formed an almost psychological force; never was a team greater than the sum of its parts like this one was. This team also conformed strongly to the culture the organization instilled from our very first day, led by Bill Foley's vision and the execution thereof by George, me, and every other person in our organization. Our culture then, and as it continues today, is the ultimate competitive advantage.

The early success completely changed the calculus of our approach. The five years since have been based on an unwavering faith that we knew what our roster needed to look like to be a sustainable contending team and, once we had grown to that point, what it would take to be a champion team. Year one was magical, but, as pleased as we were, objectively, to be a contender on a continual basis, we needed to improve our personnel. Signing free agent Paul Stastny and trading for Max Pacioretty and later Mark Stone started that process. Year

three, we traded for Chandler Stephenson, Nic Roy, Alec Martinez, and Robin Lehner while welcoming defensemen Nicolas Hague, a 2017 draft choice, and collegiate free agent Zach Whitecloud to our NHL lineup after developing in the American Hockey League.

After advancing to the Conference Final versus Dallas in 2020, it became apparent that we needed an elite No. 1 defenseman, and our focus for year four was Alex Pietrangelo, the Stanley Cup–champion captain of the St. Louis Blues. We signed Alex to a seven-year contract as free agency began, and we now had not only our D1 but also an alpha male and a tremendous leader in our locker room. In the COVID-19-shortened 2020–21 season, we finished with the most wins in the NHL, then defeated Minnesota, and then the Presidents' Trophy winners, Colorado, before losing in the third round to Montreal.

Season five, we were humbled, and I believe this helped us become champions. Despite feeling that we had our best roster to date, we were decimated by injury, losing over 500 man-games. That said, regardless of the reasons, missing the playoffs is

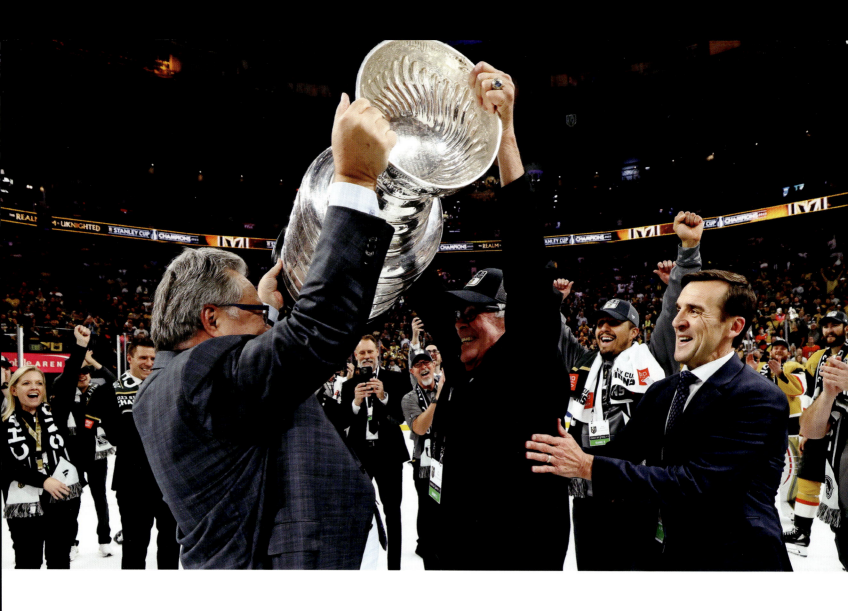

humbling, and I feel maybe we needed that. We had lost our identity a bit, and there were signs of entitlement that were concerning to George and me on the inside. Since day one, our team was at its best when we were proving people wrong. That chip on our shoulder had always served us well. Once again, we had something to prove.

In season five, we made offseason deals for Brett Howden and Nolan Patrick and retained free agent Mattias Janmark. Perhaps the most significant development that year, however, was the acquisition of star center Jack Eichel. From our conference final loss versus Montreal, we had felt that a true No. 1 center was required to win the Stanley Cup, and one need not look further than past champions to support that argument. While we were strong up the middle, we had never had that true No. 1 center, and they are incredibly hard to find. Complicating the trade discussions, Jack had a broken neck that would require surgery – a surgery that had never been performed on an NHL player before. In addition, he was making $10 million, which would have to be absorbed into our salary cap in season. We believed it was worth

the risk, however, and we completed the trade for Jack with Buffalo in early November.

Even though we missed the playoffs in 2021–22, George, our pro scouting staff, our hockey operations group, and I all felt we had assembled a team worthy of winning a Stanley Cup. From a personnel standpoint, our 2022 offseason was quiet: an under-the-radar trade to acquire goaltender Adin Hill in August upon news that Robin Lehner would miss the entire season, and the signing of free agent Phil Kessel. But the move that brought our vision to reality was the hiring of Bruce Cassidy, who was the right coach at the right time for our organization. Bruce had our team play to the identity that we envisioned, and demanded accountability. Success is rarely a straight line, however, and there was a time, as we came out of the All-Star break in early February, that playoffs were in jeopardy. But from there, we finished 22–4–5 to win the Pacific Division and the Western Conference.

Stanley Cup Playoffs are very high stakes, there are always nerves at play, and there are times when you have doubts. That is natural. But the character

IT HURTS TO WIN

Bruce Cassidy introduced the "It Hurts to Win" mantra to the Vegas Golden Knights. It started as a phrase that would creep into the occasional pregame speech or postgame press conference. It lives on now in 2023 playoff tee-shirts and the title of this book. Like so much that Bruce brought to Vegas, it rings true.

It certainly fit with the 2022–23 Vegas Golden Knights.

No Stanley Cup winning team has blocked more shots per game since the stat has been tracked. Injuries at the sport's most important position made Vegas the first team in history to etch four goaltenders' names on the Stanley Cup. And the team captain had two back surgeries in the 13 months prior to hoisting the Cup.

That's on top of the typical bumps and bruises that plague any team that endures 100-plus games in a season (Game 5 versus Florida was Vegas' 104th). While Vegas didn't lose many players from their lineup due to injury during the playoffs, that's not to say none were banged up.

As Bruce smartly noted, It Hurts to Win.

and leadership this team possessed, combined with the leadership from the coaching staff, gave one the feeling that we were well prepared and ready for the exam. The sense of calm from our players helped guide us through some tremendous challenges, defeating four high-quality hockey teams.

Someone always seized the big moments – one player did not have to do it all. Our D corps, led by Pietrangelo, along with Martinez, McNabb, Theodore, Whitecloud, and Hague, as well as Ben Hutton, was our foundation every night. At center, Eichel, Stephenson, Karlsson, and Roy gave us tremendous depth in the middle of the ice. And Jonathan Marchessault and Mark Stone are two of the best big-game players in the NHL. A trade deadline acquisition of Ivan Barbashev gave us something we were missing, and the goaltending was great all season, with Logan Thompson becoming an All-Star, Laurent Brossoit and Adin Hill leading us through the playoffs, and Jonathan Quick providing even more leadership in an already strong dressing room.

I refer back to the unwavering faith of our management and scouting staff. We knew exactly what a championship team needed to look like, and we had the resolve to shut out the noise. Only we truly knew our team and our plan. We stuck with both. We were a team that had been in 11 playoff series prior to this year, and we have now played in

15, winning 11 of those. I am proud that we forged ahead with our beliefs, and it was special to win with our hockey operations staff, which had been together from the outset. Our final roster was composed of 11 players acquired through trade, seven free agents, six Misfits, two draft choices, and one player selected off waivers.

The other aspect of this is how hard it is to build a team the way we did. There was a great deal of personal cost; we made many hard decisions on very good people. That is not easy. When you care about people and appreciate what they have done, it is even harder. I do not want that to go unsaid, because it's a hard journey to build a championship team. I also know that our players appreciate that we are trying to win – that is what it is all about.

Get ready to read about this journey through the eyes of the people who did it: the players. I have so much respect for these players, their character, their toughness, their selflessness to each other. Seeing the sheer joy in their faces on the ice after we won is a feeling I will never forget.

Enjoy!

A NEW START

After missing the playoffs for the first time in franchise history, the Vegas Golden Knights entered 2022-23 with a new head coach and a drive to return to the standard of excellence the franchise had set in its first four seasons.

The ice has melted. Championship ice. Gone forever. But the memories created are eternal.

There are 32 NHL franchises. Only 21 have won the Stanley Cup. The Golden Knights are now on that celebrated list.

Bill Foley's team needed just six seasons to win hockey's iconic trophy. You remember, Bill said, "Cup in six," before his team ever played a game. Yes, "Cup in six." Just like the man said.

The Golden Knights' 9–3 win in Game 5 of the final clinched a 4–1 series victory over the Florida Panthers. Jonathan Marchessault's 13 goals and 25 points earned him the Conn Smythe Trophy as playoff MVP.

And moments after Commissioner Gary Bettman awarded the trophy to original Golden Misfit Marchessault, VGK captain Mark Stone was summoned to lift the Stanley Cup over his head. The witnesses: his rapt teammates, 19,058 Medieval Maniacs in T-Mobile Arena, and Golden Knights fans across Nevada and the globe.

Later, Stone would scream, "We're the best hockey team in the world!" as his teammates hosed him down with champagne in a jubilant dressing room.

Since entering the NHL, the Golden Knights rank fifth in regular-season wins (267), and second in playoff wins (54) to the Tampa Bay Lightning (61). Only Tampa Bay (13) has won more playoff rounds than Vegas (11).

Bruce Cassidy held practices in three groups for each of the first three days of his first Golden Knights training camp, which began September 22.

The team appeared poised to make a deep playoff run in the 2021–22 season, but a historic wave of injuries resulted in Vegas missing the playoffs.

Some called for Vegas to scrap the roster and rebuild. McCrimmon and McPhee retooled and doubled down on their core. The result: hockey history in the desert.

+ + + + + +

KELLY MCCRIMMON We were disappointed at the end of the 2021–22 season because we made a push to get in the playoffs as the season winded down. That is probably the overriding feeling – you do a thorough analysis of everything that went into that situation and how you got there, and what you want to address, what you want to try to change.

BILL FOLEY Missing the playoffs in 2021–22 was really disappointing. The hockey staff decided to make a coaching change, which I was in agreement with. I felt like we needed to move in a different direction going forward with a different style, and a different relationship between the coach and the players. We made a terrific move bringing in Butch Cassidy, and it was flawless.

In six seasons, the franchise, directed by hockey czars George McPhee and Kelly McCrimmon, has made the playoffs five times and the conference final on four occasions. Twice, the Golden Knights have competed in the Stanley Cup Final, losing to the Washington Capitals in the team's first NHL season and defeating Florida in year six.

In 2022–23, the VGK won 51 regular-season games and captured both the Pacific Division and Western Conference regular-season titles. Playoff-round victories over the Winnipeg Jets, the Edmonton Oilers, and the Dallas Stars preceded the Final.

A season for the ages. But, as McCrimmon said in a postgame interview, "We didn't jump the fence. We've had good teams here for a while."

MCCRIMMON The exit meetings are always important – maybe more so after a year like that. I felt we had lost our identity somewhat. I thought we'd always benefited from an attitude that we carried with us from day one: We had something to prove, and we were looking to prove people wrong.

We knew we needed to get that back. I thought that our older players needed to be more accountable than I felt they had been. It wasn't so much about the 2021–22 season as it was about the 2022–23 season.

We were in a position where we were going to have a long offseason. We had a lot of players that needed some time to recover. And in my opinion, I felt part of starting fresh in the fall was going to include some changes to our coaching staff.

BRUCE CASSIDY I was new, so I was trying to take in as much as I could. The players that I talked

to were predominantly good. There were a couple that spoke their minds a little more about how they felt they needed certain things to be tightened up – playing as a team, accountability, and those types of areas. I read Max Pacioretty's comments when he went out the door that it was like a country club, or something to that effect. I talked to Mark Stone – he said that we need to make sure we're all on the same page and get back to that. He wasn't critical of the room – he just felt they needed to get back to where they had previously been.

I had to decipher what that meant. I talked to Ryan Craig and Kelly McCrimmon about that. That's one of the reasons I was hired – they felt that I could do that for a team. I didn't go outside of the organization. I went inside and got the information I needed.

People talk about accountability. There are different ways you can enforce that: What is accountability? Is it puck management? Is it shift length? To me,

it's a lot of different things. That's what we figured we'd do right out of the gate. We did – we held our ground on that. It didn't matter if you were the best player – the twelfth forward or the first forward.

JACK EICHEL Bruce pushed guys when they didn't want to be pushed this year. I think he didn't let anyone off the hook. He held the entire group extremely accountable, and you knew where you stood with him the whole year.

I think that was good for me, and that was something I needed. At times, I probably didn't love it, but looking back, I think it made me a better player. He did a lot for me, and he did a lot for our whole team. He was very good with his details in the game and teaching those details and getting us to play a certain way.

JONATHAN MARCHESSAULT Well, to be honest, Bruce and I had some pretty good battles this year, both on the bench and behind closed doors.

WELCOME, BRUCE

If your phone buzzed on June 7, 2022, to alert you that Bruce Cassidy had been fired as head coach of the Boston Bruins, you probably had to look at it twice to make sure you read it correctly.

After posting a 245-108-46 record in six seasons behind the Boston bench, the coach who led the Bruins to the 2019 Stanley Cup Final became available. The Vegas Golden Knights had moved on from Pete DeBoer just three weeks earlier and were searching for a coach who could turn a contender into a champion.

Nine days after his departure from Boston, Cassidy was announced as the head coach of the Golden Knights. On a hot day in June, he flew to Vegas, met some of the staff at Red Rock Casino, Resort & Spa, walked across the street to City National Arena, and settled into his new home. Alongside General Manager Kelly McCrimmon, Cassidy told the media that he came to Vegas for one reason – to chase the Stanley Cup.

It was there that he learned about Bill Foley's brave words from 2016, when he had predicted that the team would win the Stanley Cup within six years.

"We're in year six, right? So the pressure's on, which is great," Cassidy said with a smile in his first media session in Vegas. "You want to be relevant, and you want expectations. I think we're all aware they're out there, and I'm here to fulfill them."

External expectations for the Golden Knights were mixed after the team failed to qualify for the Stanley Cup Playoffs for the first time in franchise history in 2021-22. McCrimmon had a list of things he was looking for in the next bench boss for his team.

"He embodies so many of the traits that we were looking for," McCrimmon said at Cassidy's introductory press conference. "He has a great record of success. Any way you want to measure performance of a team, his teams have been extremely successful. It's a real opportunity for the Golden Knights. I think it makes our team better. It only adds to the success that we have heading into this coming season."

Just 364 days later, Cassidy hoisted the Stanley Cup at center ice at T-Mobile Arena.

After the Golden Knights captured the sport's ultimate prize, George McPhee,

president of hockey operations, shared a story from the week the team hired Cassidy in Vegas. McCrimmon had asked Mark Stone to call Bruins captain Patrice Bergeron to ask him about Cassidy.

"I guess they had their conversation," McPhee said. "And at the end of the call, Patrice said, 'Holy smokes. Vegas is going to hire Bruce Cassidy, and they're going to win the Stanley Cup next year.'"

At the same time, his desire to win is as big as my desire to win. He's a winner – he won it in the first year with us. He's a winner, and I'm a winner. That's something that no one can take away from us.

I thought he was a really good coach – definitely hard sometimes on certain guys. Not that I would agree with everything, but at the same time, I'm a player and he's a coach. One day, when I'll be a coach or GM, it's going to be my ship. I'm going to run it the way I want to run it. Right now, it's his ship, and he runs it the way he wants to run it. That's something that I definitely agree with. Everybody can argue about certain decisions, but he won it. You can't second-guess a guy that just won.

ALEX PIETRANGELO We missed the playoffs the year before, and the first thing I said to my wife was, "This is a great opportunity – not only for me,

but also for other guys, to get some rest. This is a huge opportunity." Think about how many years in a row I've made the playoffs – to get that much time off mentally was, for me, great. We kind of got an opportunity to mentally get away, physically get away.

ALEC MARTINEZ Last season was good for us in a lot of ways. It's easy to say now, but we needed to get knocked down to size a little bit. Not even making the playoffs, while it was disappointing, you could use it as an opportunity for a lot of different things – reflecting on your own game, the team game, getting healthy, and things like that. You could embrace it, and I think that the guys did.

MARK STONE I think there was actually a lot of confidence because management and ownership, they could have gone a different way. Missing the

playoffs for the first time, they could have given up on the group. But they showed a lot of confidence in us.

We were just confident because we knew we were going to get another opportunity at it. And we had that defiant mentality coming in. I think a lot of people were counting on our downfall, said we were done. Said we were too old, or made too many moves, or whatever it was. But we were ready to go right from the first day of training camp. Guys were here early, and I think that showed the confidence that guys were ready to go.

WILLIAM KARLSSON You hear people talking about blowing up the team and going into a rebuild and those sorts of things. We felt if we had squeaked into the playoffs and then got healthy, we could be a dangerous team. It never happened.

But that doesn't take away from this roster. It's the NHL, and every team can win. It's a fine line. People who never watched us or didn't understand how all those injuries affected us had opinions that we felt were off base. We've all been told things before in our careers – been labeled a certain way. And we've all proven those things to be false.

EICHEL The only thing that mattered to me was getting to the playoffs. Last summer, that was it. I didn't care about what happened statistically. I just have to be a part of the playoffs – our team has to make the playoffs. I wrote down a million goals, but the main goal was just to get to the playoffs.

STONE Bruce is coming to a brand-new team, and a team that's only been in the league for five years, with the expectation to win. I think that's probably

OPPOSITE
Nicolas Roy produced his second-straight 30-point season in 2022–23.

ABOVE
Logan Thompson (left) and Adin Hill combined to start the first 56 games of the season for Vegas, posting a joint 34-18-4 record in that time.

why he took the job. That's probably why he fit in, and he addressed that early. Practices were up-tempo from the get-go.

I think we had to do some adapting to him, but he had to do some adapting to us. We obviously have a very different locker room than probably what Boston was. We have quite a few personalities in our locker room – we like to have a good time. I think it took him a little bit of time to realize that we do have fun, but we also know when it's time to go. So as the season went along, our relationships as players and coaching staff got a lot stronger.

He's not easy – accountability is his big thing. Sometimes it comes across maybe sarcastic or brash. He's an emotional guy. He wears his heart on his sleeve. You can see it behind the bench. He doesn't want to be yelling all game, but he cares so much.

I think there was this cloud over this team that everything was easy. I think he came in thinking

that. But guys like accountability – we hold each other accountable. Ultimately, we like to have fun as a team – we like to enjoy each other's company. And if you're not having fun, I don't think you're going to have a lot of success, because the most fun thing to do is win. And that's what we wanted to do.

CASSIDY Training camp was important to establish work ethic and teach the system as well. I thought we were real organized with that, and effective. A number of people upstairs who were hockey guys who watched it told me that they liked the way it was done. It was progressive, and we still got our work in and our touches – the players even said that.

That part was good, and I thought our preseason was solid. Not great, not bad, but we got better. The next part was winning, and we got off to the right foot. My guess is that they thought I was coming in with a sledgehammer. I wouldn't say a

sledgehammer, not so much, but he's coming in and not letting them get away with anything. That was the plan, and that's what I was basically asked to do.

MARTINEZ His mentality was really good for us. There was a lot of learning – not that it ever stops – but I think that there was a lot of learning on both sides at the beginning. I think Butch learned toward the end to trust us a little bit as a group and as a leadership group. At the beginning of the year, I think that he was trying to figure out what kind of group he was inheriting and what tweaks needed to be made.

There was a general feeling around the league that we were entitled, we didn't do the right things, and we didn't work hard enough. There were some things said in the media and stuff last summer. From an outsider's perspective, I don't know how anyone else's locker room works unless you're in it.

He kept us accountable, which was really good. I thought he brought intensity in practice and on the bench. That was really good as well.

The main thing is that he started to trust us a little bit. I always knew that we had a really good group. There were some things that, in terms of mentality, we had to tweak or change.

Bruce's demeanor and mentality gave us a little bit of a nudge. This is no disrespect to anyone else, but maybe we don't win without Bruce. His demeanor certainly helped out a lot. Both sides learned a lot toward the end of the year. Obviously, it was a recipe for success.

It's hard for me to say this stuff because I don't want to disrespect Pete DeBoer, and I don't want to disrespect the guys that were in the locker room before.

ALEX PIETRANGELO First of all, his system is completely different. It's like nothing I've ever played. At first it was like, OK, is this going to work? You're always wondering in your head – "This is completely different."

CASSIDY Coaching styles are interesting because sometimes what the players feel your style is versus

OPPOSITE
Michael Amadio enjoyed the best season of his career, posting 16 goals and 11 assists in 67 games.

ABOVE
Logan Thompson posted a shutout of Chicago in the home opener. His 8-2-0 record in November earned NHL Rookie of the Month honors.

33

MONTANA TEAM BUILDING

Every team carves out time during training camp for the players and staff to bond as a group. Most teams will do a group dinner, have a golf outing, spend time in nature, or some other activity where everyone comes together for the sole purpose of creating chemistry.

Bill Foley makes sure the annual gathering for his Vegas Golden Knights includes all of that and more. He opens the barn doors at the Rock Creek Cattle Company for his players to golf on his Top 100-rated course, dine in the property's top-end restaurant, explore the 30,000-acre property on horseback, ATV and boat, all under Montana's big sky.

In early October, the team made its yearly trip during a break in preseason action. Veterans of the team had visited in the past, but Jack Eichel was among the first-timers on the trip ahead of the 2022-23 season.

"That trip was enormous," Eichel said. "It was the first time the group was together by ourselves and really built chemistry. You get that from Halloween parties or rookie dinners, but doing it before the first game of the season is special. It really jump-started things for us."

The time spent at Rock Creek symbolizes more than a break from hockey. It's even bigger than a one-off trip for that year's team to come together. When the Golden Knights head up to the ranch each year, friendships are cemented that last far beyond the end of that season. Annual traditions like poker tournaments and late-night swims become legend for every Golden Knight who makes the trip.

When the 2022-23 Golden Knights returned from the Rock Creek Cattle Company, the first step in a season-long journey to greatness was taken.

what the coach feels doesn't always match up. I've always felt I was a guy that – demanding is a strong word, but I think it's a good word in certain instances in terms of the expectation. You have to be *demanding* to meet that at times.

Accountability. I also felt that I allowed players to have a lot of creativity, so I thought my coaching style would be just fine. You got a bunch of veteran guys who want to win who have been close – myself included. I believe in good team defense, and I think this team certainly has those qualities in them and had shown that in the past. Some creativity to score, I think, was where the team had got bogged down over the years – the ability to get inside, and how you're going to score.

That's part of your coaching style and your coaching beliefs, I guess, so I thought that would be fine with this group. But you don't know how to get into it. And as we went along, we obviously were able to connect with the players and get it done.

JACK EICHEL With Bruce, it really wasn't about how we're going to play a certain way. It was more so that we have to be ready to play when the puck drops at the beginning of the game.

It was early in the year – I think we were playing Colorado at home. I didn't have a great first period, and he came in the locker room and he said a few things. I let it go, but I didn't like the way that he handled it. I didn't say anything to him at the time. I actually just went in and spoke with him the next day and told him that I didn't have any problem with him holding me accountable. I just think there's a way to do it. I said, "I don't like the idea of you trying to embarrass me in front of the team." He said, "That's not why I did it," and that he wasn't trying to embarrass me. I said, "I felt like you were. I have no problem with you holding me accountable. You can yell at me – I'm a big boy." There's a way to do things and there's a way not to, and we had a good conversation.

It started to take off from there because he understood what I needed from him. I don't mind a kick in the ass. We hashed it out, and things went well. Early in the season, and I think he was trying to figure everyone out. He got into it with a lot of other guys more than me.

PIETRANGELO When the season started, we came out on fire. We came out fresh.

WILLIAM KARLSSON We started out great. Won 13 of our first 15 games. We got our belief back. We needed it. Camp was hard but good. We all worked out hard in the offseason and came to camp ready to go. The fun was back too. We had some anger about the previous season. But it was like the room had fresh air in it.

I AM IRONMAN

If you watched Phil Kessel gear up for a game in 2023, you'd wonder if certain pieces of his equipment were part of his ensemble on November 3, 2009. It was on that day that Kessel made his Toronto Maple Leafs debut and the longest consecutive-games-played streak in NHL history began.

On October 25, 2022, Kessel's mixture of beat-up gear and more modern hockey protection was strapped onto his body as he suited up for his NHL-record 990th consecutive game. Kessel spent 13 straight years avoiding injuries, dips in play, and even an entire pandemic as his name was on his team's lineup card every night. He said there were plenty of close calls throughout the years, but his desire to play never wavered.

After tying Keith Yandle's record of 989 straight games the night before, Kessel broke the record during his first shift at SAP Center as the Vegas Golden Knights visited the San Jose Sharks for the team's eighth game of the year.

From the stands, Phil Kessel Sr. watched his son employ the same mentality he's had

from the start: If you're paid to do a job, you had better show up and do it.

"I've got to watch my kid play way past his youth days, and it's been nice for me because we've had the experience and we get to follow him around," Kessel Sr. said. "It gives us something else to think about."

The NHL's Ironman record wasn't the only slice of hockey history Kessel had on his plate that night. In the first period, he broke behind the San Jose defense and lifted his 400th NHL goal into the top left corner of the cage. Kessel became the 13th US-born player to join the 400-goal

club as he helped Vegas to a 4-2 win against the Sharks.

"That's how it works, right?" Kessel said. "It's a special night for me, it all worked out."

Kessel's night ended with a game puck from Mark Stone and a chant of "Phil! Phil! Phil! Phil!" echoing through the visitors' dressing room. The team welcomed the veteran forward with open arms from the beginning, but it was that night in San Jose that cemented Kessel as a Vegas Golden Knight.

"It's just a blessing," Kessel said. "I've loved every minute of it."

PIETRANGELO I think the thing that helped us the most as a group and probably Bruce as a coach was having success early because it allowed everybody to get on the same page and get on board to trust the system. If a new coach comes in and has a system implemented and it doesn't work, then nobody wants to follow it. We had so much success early on it was, like, "OK, this is going to work – this is good for our group."

Was it perfect? No. It probably took us 30 or 40 games to really have it become second nature for us. But we had success early, and I think that allowed everybody to be, like, "OK, let's get on the same page. This is something that could work for us."

MARCHESSAULT We came through for one another this season. We won for Jack the night we were in Buffalo. He was awesome, getting the hat trick and everything, but it was a team win. You could tell the way the guys mobbed him on the ice.

And he was emotional in the room after. It was a good moment for all of us – a building block for our team.

And we went into Boston – they were the best team in the league at that time, but we were right behind them, and we won for Bruce. We knew what it meant to him. And he was new to our group, but that's what we were like this year. We played for one another all the time. Same with Phil. We barely knew him, but we all felt part of his streak and wanted it to happen with a win. That night in the dressing room in San Jose, the picture with everyone around him – that was the start of some really good things happening for individuals but shared as a group thing.

EICHEL That night in Buffalo, up until then in my NHL career, I'd never felt more part of a team. Winning in the playoffs and getting the Cup has happened since. But the way the guys showed up that night and helped me through it, it was amazing.

OPPOSITE
Jack Eichel's first hat trick as a Golden Knight came in his return to Buffalo on November 10.

GOAL
ORIENTED

BY JACK EICHEL

Each offseason, I write down goals for the year ahead. I take it seriously: I give it a lot of thought and then sit down, remove any distractions, and put them all down on paper.

This list of goals isn't something that I share with people, but I can let you know the main thing I was focused on in the summer of 2022: Get to the playoffs.

That summed it up. There was a lot I wanted to achieve – and, sure, the Stanley Cup is always on your mind as a hockey player. But one step at a time.

When I got traded to Vegas in 2021, I figured I'd make my first shot at the playoffs. You never take something like that for granted – especially not after missing the playoffs for the first six years of my career – but looking at the roster, I thought it was coming. After all, the team had never missed the playoffs, which was one of the things that made Vegas so appealing.

Looking back now, I think the sting of missing the playoffs that spring really set us up for success. When guys got back in town before training camp, there was a real feeling of excitement. Nobody on

the outside seemed to give us much of a chance, which helped bring us all together even more. It was a close room of good guys when I got here, but there was even more cohesion now.

As Bruce Cassidy started implementing his system, it became pretty clear what a smart hockey mind he had. And, credit to our group, we picked it up quickly.

We got the big opening night win, fittingly, when Mark Stone scored late. Then we come back home and it's the young guys – Paul Cotter and Logan Thompson – who lead the way. Win one more and we're 3–0–0, and the belief in ourselves had really caught hold. We had come to camp thinking we could be pretty good – now we knew we were that team, and that confidence made us even tougher to beat.

Along the way, you had Phil Kessel break the Ironman record, and a milestone like that – especially when it's a guy, like Phil, who everybody

loves – can be really meaningful. Then we hit the road and won four more in a row, including two in overtime.

That put us at 12–2–0 headed back to Buffalo on November 10. That confidence, and the bond we had built, had me feeling positive, but we all knew how our last visit had gone – it was one of the toughest nights, if not the toughest, in my career.

What sticks with me about this visit was how much the rest of the guys wanted that game. We didn't talk about it much, but they all knew what it meant to me. When I got an assist, Stoney celebrated like I had scored in overtime.

Getting the last three goals for my first Vegas hat trick was fun, of course, but what I remember was the feeling in the room - it felt like another milestone, in a way. We were 13–2–0, and we'd already had some significant moments.

That start really set us up for what was ahead. There was a ways to go, but "playoffs" seemed like a goal that was going to get checked off – and bigger things beyond that started to seem possible.

THE TEAM

It takes multiple elements to create a Stanley Cup-winning roster. Vegas leaders worked for years to assemble a lineup that featured depth, size, and some of the NHL's best players at critical positions.

Most Stanley Cup champions collapse at the finish line after winning sixteen playoff games. Not the 2022–23 Vegas Golden Knights.

Drenched in joy and champagne, they felt was a palpable sense of freshness.

"Who's next?" was a popular sentiment. This team felt it could go another round.

And though Jonathan Marchessault was awarded the Conn Smythe Trophy, any number of players would have been worthy recipients: Jack Eichel, William Karlsson, Mark Stone, Adin Hill, and Alex Pietrangelo all had MVP-type playoffs.

The team was built around certain key elements: Deep and balanced. Strong on the blueline and up the middle with elite players like Stone, Eichel, and Pietrangelo at key positions.

Goaltending was the only question mark heading into the season. Vegas had a largely untested trio of Hill, Logan Thompson, and Laurent Brossoit – a question mark that would get answered over and over.

From the moment Vegas lost to the Capitals to end year one, the organization continued to search for a championship mix of talent and character.

+ + + + + +

WILLIAM CARRIER It's the best team I've ever played on. Looking back, we beat some pretty solid teams. I wouldn't say it was easy, but Stoney would finish a playoff game sometimes playing 14 minutes, and I'd be at the same number as him. Normally, these top guys in the playoffs are grinding and playing with injuries and playing 25 minutes a night, and it did not feel like that all playoffs. I think some guys could have played an extra round.

Alex Pietrangelo led the Golden Knights in ice time for the third year in a row and established a club record for points by a defenseman (54).

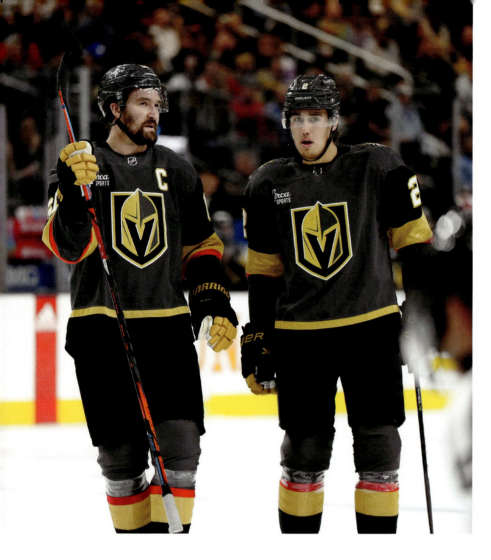

Team captain Mark Stone (left) had few new charges in the 2022-23 locker room, with players like Zach Whitecloud now a regular for the third year.

I think it's the best team by far – the most depth I've had. I feel like we had no weaknesses, really. I think the only thing we had to work on was just consistency, and if we did the same thing night after night, we'd be all right. We saw it when the team put it together – we're a pretty solid team.

KELLY MCCRIMMON We were good in year one, but we felt if we were going to be a contending team, we needed to improve. We were always trying to make our team better. We got Mark Stone, who quickly became our natural leader and then our first captain. We really wanted to see if we could add a No. 1 defenseman based on what, in our view, Stanley Cup champion teams look like. And that was the motivation behind the signing of Alex Pietrangelo. We also came to understand we needed a pure first-line center. And we started working on the trade for Jack Eichel.

GEORGE MCPHEE The challenge is always that we had great chemistry with that year one team. Chemistry is a really elusive thing. You either have it or you don't, and it's hard to manufacture. So we knew we needed to be a better team, but taking

pieces out of that team to do it was going to be a difficult process. And it was, but like everything else we've done, the organization comes first and the individual comes a close second.

It's how we manage everything we do – as long as you're being honest and straight with the players, and you're doing what's best for the organization. People can call it what they want, but we're doing what's best to ultimately win. We didn't want to take away too much from that team. But we had to start understanding that if we were going to win, we needed upgrades in certain areas.

BRUCE CASSIDY Kelly doesn't get enough credit. We were at the NHL Draft and all the general managers were congratulating him. Thanks to Nashville for hosting the draft, and congratulations to Vegas for winning. Then, the crowd there would always boo. Why are we hated so much? I've only been here for a year, but I imagine there is a certain amount of jealousy because of how good the team was so quickly.

At the end of the day, Kelly is a very smart hockey guy. When I talk to him about the roster, we align in terms of how we want to play, our strengths, down the middle, D core – the things that I also believe in. He has done a terrific job. From the outside, again, sometimes it looks like he got rid of all the popular guys to do it. That's business sometimes. If you want to win, those are the decisions that you have to make, especially with a hard cap.

I didn't look at it that way, I just looked at it as a guy that's willing to make hard decisions for the good of the team. If you're OK with that as a player, a coach, and someone that's working for the team, then it's a great place for you. If you're a little more sentimental, then maybe it won't be.

ALEC MARTINEZ It's up to the guys in the room, but it's also up to the heads of the organization to put the right guys in that room. It all needs to work together. There is a certain element of everyone needing to be on the same page. Then, there's also the element where I'm a player, I'm not the GM. It's partially my duty to just be a good soldier and put my head down, but knowing that management

FROM SURGERY TO SURGICAL

Jack Eichel's time with the Buffalo Sabres had more downs than ups, as the center's six seasons with the Sabres after being selected second overall in 2015 yielded no playoff appearances. He suffered a neck injury and went through a dispute with the Sabres about treatment that dragged on for six months.

Eichel began to write a new chapter when he was traded to the Vegas Golden Knights in November 2021. He became the first NHL player to receive artificial disk-replacement surgery just days after being introduced as the newest Golden Knight at a press conference at City National Arena. He spent three months away from the team on the mend following guidance from his doctor and the Vegas medical staff.

On January 11, 2022, he walked into the team's practice facility in Summerlin to find his locker stall set up for his first organized skate with the Golden Knights. He donned a red noncontact jersey and received a chorus of cheers from fans at City National Arena as he took his first step on the ice to practice with the team.

One month later, Eichel was cleared to play for the first time since March 7, 2021. He made his Golden Knights debut against the Colorado Avalanche and, two games later, scored his first goal with his new team against the San Jose Sharks.

Eichel finished the 2021-22 season with 25 points (14 goals, 11 assists) in 34 games. He shared in the team's disappointment when the Stanley Cup Playoffs began and

the Golden Knights became spectators. While that season left a bitter taste in the center's mouth, the sweetness of returning from injury and receiving a fresh start allowed him to look excitedly toward 2022-23.

"We would've liked to have had more success," Eichel said at the end of the 2021-22 campaign. "I know we will."

The injury bug's bite didn't have quite the same force for Eichel in his second season with the Golden Knights, as he appeared in 67 of the team's 82 games. His 66 points (27 goals, 39 assists) topped Vegas' scoring chart and helped the team win the Pacific Division title.

Doubters and haters were disappointed when Eichel realized his dream of playing in the Stanley Cup Playoffs. The opportunity to prove himself on the postseason stage was one that Eichel made the absolute most of as he played a pivotal role in the first Stanley Cup championship in Golden Knights history.

Eichel led all skaters in the playoffs with 26 points (6 goals, 20 assists) and was runner-up to linemate Jonathan Marchessault in voting for the Conn Smythe Trophy as the most valuable player in the postseason. He finished behind only Mark Recchi (1991) and Eric Staal (2006) in scoring by a player who was playing in the Stanley Cup Playoffs for the first time.

After getting his hands on the Stanley Cup, Eichel was able to put his journey into perspective.

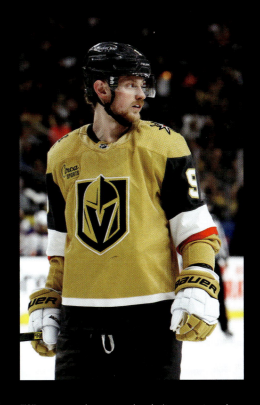

"When you take a step back, it was a tough time, for sure," Eichel said. "I can't lie – it sucked not playing and having uncertainty about my future. Vegas took a chance and believed in me and what I wanted to do. It is all worth it now. I'm a Stanley Cup Champion with this group, this organization, this town. All the stuff you go through is worth it. When you go through situations like that, it changes your perspective on things. I think I matured a lot through that whole process, and it allowed me to succeed. I just can't say enough about Bill Foley, George McPhee, Kelly McCrimmon, the medical staff here – these people are the reason that I'm here."

is going to give you the best possible chance to take a run at it, I think that's really important.

Morale is a big thing. If guys don't believe in the group that's putting the team together, that's certainly going to hurt.

MCPHEE It's one of the pillars of this team. When we first put it together, it was, yes, we want talent. Yes, we want good hockey IQ. Yes, we want good skating. All of those things, but the most important attributes are leadership and character

and compete. We've had a lot of that from day one. Before we ever put a team on the ice, that's what we wanted in the players. That has stayed with this organization for all six years.

MARK STONE This organization was ready to do whatever it took to win. That's why I wanted to be where I am right now. It's tough to lose teammates. It really is. We lost a lot of good people – a lot of good friends – along this road to build the team that we went to battle with this year. And a lot of fan favorites from that first year – that first year was special.

But in a salary cap and just in pro sports in general, you're never going to bring the same team back. I'm sure if you asked them, they probably traded some people they didn't want to trade, but to add a No. 1 defenseman, to add a No. 1 center, it comes at a price. A lot of teams aren't willing to do that.

I guess everybody thinks you draft them, you develop them, you keep them. We've only been drafting since 2017. It's hard to get those guys, and I think that's what this organization has done. They've watched teams that win and they have a No. 1 center, they have a No. 1 defenseman, they're deep down the middle with great goaltending as well. I love that the organization – especially now, I love that the organization did everything they could to win, because I'm sitting here a Stanley Cup champion.

MCCRIMMON Jack Eichel is a tremendous talent. He's an elite-level skater – his skill set, his puck handling, his shooting, his vision, his passing are very, very high end. I think him coming in on day one this season, healthy and in tremendous condition, was important – then the transformation, or the way that his game evolved this past season.

The Jack Eichel that we talk about now is a tremendous player, he's a winner, he's a champion, he has great competitiveness. I thought this playoff, he was fantastic in so many ways: his skating ability, to track pucks, reload, snuff out plays defensively, timely offense, transition, get the puck up the ice, hold the puck, make plays. He's a star. And he is an extremely respected teammate. His work ethic is second to none. He's the first guy on the ice. He's the last guy off.

OPPOSITE
Jack Eichel led the team in points with 66, just one shy of averaging a point per game.

ABOVE
A leadership group that included (left to right) Mark Stone, Alex Pietrangelo, and Alec Martinez gave Vegas a significant veteran presence.

JONATHAN MARCHESSAULT Jack's a game changer. He turns on the jets and changes the game on his own. Every time he gets the puck on the ice, something special is probably going to happen. He's the kind of guy that makes everybody better out there, like Mark Stone. It's impressive to see, to be honest. I think he's electric.

He's probably one of the guys that I'm most happy for because he got so much criticism when he left Buffalo – the way Buffalo fans treated him and all that after. A lot of people used to say you don't win with a guy like Jack, and look at him right now. He's a Stanley Cup winner at 26 years old. It's pretty impressive, and good for him. I'm so proud and happy for him because of all the haters he has.

MARTINEZ Let's start with Stone, with him being the captain. That guy, he is the ultimate competitor. He is probably one of the most competitive guys that I've ever played with. The guy just genuinely

cares – he wants to win. He's willing to do whatever it takes to reach that pinnacle. It's no secret, with some of the injury troubles that he's had. Seeing a guy like that and the work that he put in just to put himself in that position, it's pretty remarkable. To do what he did in the playoffs, coming off of a procedure like that, that's wild. That's why he's the captain of our hockey club.

I was on the team before he was named captain. He was the obvious choice, and I don't think anyone came close. He's a leader. He puts in the work on and off the ice. He says the right things. People respect him when he speaks up, people listen, he knows the right thing to say at the right time. He was the guy for the job.

MCCRIMMON Mark Stone is a tremendous NHL player. He is appreciated the more you watch him – he makes others around him better. His positive impact on teammates' play is such a big part of

ALL-STAR SELECTIONS

One year after the Vegas Golden Knights hosted the NHL All-Star Weekend at T-Mobile Arena, the team sent three All-Stars to the annual event in South Florida to represent the organization among the league's brightest stars.

On the ice, Chandler Stephenson and Logan Thompson were selected to join the Pacific Division squad. Bruce Cassidy stood behind the bench for the festivities as the head coach of the top team in the division at the break.

Stephenson and Thompson donned the Golden Knights Reverse Retro uniforms and hit the ice on the first day of the weekend for the NHL All-Stars Skills. Stephenson participated in the Fastest Skater competition and circled the ice in 14.197 seconds to place third in the competition. Thompson teamed up with Oilers goalie Stuart Skinner in the Tendy Tandem event, which saw the Vegas netminder face breakaways from Central Division shooters.

While neither Golden Knight took home hardware from the event, the duo proved they belong among the NHL's elite.

The Pacific Division dropped the first game of the 3-on-3 tournament to the Central Division and bowed out of the festivities, but Cassidy, Stephenson, and Thompson banked memories with their families that they'll carry forever.

---

what he brings to the table. Emotional leader. He is a great player, great playmaker, big, long, great at takeaways, all of those kinds of things. That would be Stone.

BRAYDEN MCNABB The best way I can describe Stoney as a player is, if you watch a game up top, it's very slow and very easy to see what plays should be made. He's the one who's always making that play, but at ice level. That's what I always say about him.

He's so intelligent. It's incredible. I'm sure he'll be a GM one day in this league. He's a very, very smart hockey mind. He does a lot of little things defensively as well. He steals pucks. His hand-eye coordination is the best I've ever seen. He's a different player, for sure. And we're very fortunate. He's turned into an unbelievable captain.

MCCRIMMON Petro is an alpha male, natural leader, steady as a rock. John Stevens would tell you he's never seen a player more even keeled, never

rattled, a calming influence on our team and our defense corps. Tremendous presence on the ice. Just an exceptional NHL defenseman.

ADIN HILL Petro's skill set is unique in the league. He's great in the D zone, great in the O zone, good on the power play – he's just kind of good at everything. He's an awesome guy to be around too. He's got two Cups with two different teams. It is pretty impressive, what he's done with his career and how he's able to elevate his game when he needs to. He is competitive, and he makes passes that I just haven't seen made before. He'll come out of our D zone and throw backhand sauce, or pass to the far blue line, and it lands on the guy's tape – didn't even touch the ice before. I don't know how he does that.

MARTINEZ I've said it a hundred times, but Petro is a horse. He does all the work, he plays big minutes, he plays physically, and he plays both ends of the rink. The guy is a physical freak. I've played with him

OPPOSITE
Bruce Cassidy's second NHL All-Star Game appearance coincided with the first selections for Golden Knights Chandler Stephenson and Logan Thompson.

players. When you add Jack in at the front of that line, it becomes a really deep group that now is the strength of your team.

STONE People don't understand how good our centers are. Obviously, Jack is our best player, and he's become one of the best two-way centers in the NHL. Chandler, what did we give up for him? A fifth-round pick? He's one of best skaters in the NHL, and we sure have found some chemistry together. I love playing with him. Karly is just so underrated. Look who he played against in the playoffs. He shut down the best every team had to offer, and he continued to produce. Nic Roy isn't a fourth-line center. He provides so much for us on that line. Any team in the NHL would love to have our fourth line.

CASSIDY The whole Eichel line got hot at the right time, and they made plays for one another all over the ice. That wasn't one guy with pucks just finding him. It was a line that really made plays for each other. Most of those goals were a result of touches from all of them in some way, shape, or form. It was just good, complementary hockey for that line.

JACK EICHEL It took Marchessault and me a bit to get our chemistry. We had played together a bit last year, but it wasn't like it was just recently. We played together a little bit this year, and we were trying to find it. After the All-Star break, I think we started to get better.

If we could get a guy like Barbie, we thought we would start having more success. When Marchessault started to build that confidence and he was playing at another level – and the same thing for Barbashev – it just felt like every night, we were going to go out there and make a few plays and help our team win. That's what we did.

Barbashev is such an easy player to play with. I remember Kelly saying to me before the deadline that they wanted to get him because we could play him anywhere. We can play him on our top line, play him on our bottom line, and we can play him middle or wing. He's like a Swiss Army knife. He has really underrated skill and hockey IQ. He makes a lot of plays that you'd be surprised about, and he's easy to play with.

ABOVE
Ivan Barbashev's addition brought Vegas a physical presence and a scoring touch, as he posted 16 points in 23 games down the stretch.

OPPOSITE
Adin Hill established career highs in games (27) and wins (16) in his first Vegas season.

for, what, three years now? I think I've heard him say on the bench that he's really tired about twice. I am pretty close with Petro, and he has been really good to me personally. When can you say your defensive partner is one of your best friends? The guy embraces it – he knows he's a No. 1 defenseman, he's a generational talent. The guy is big, he's skilled, he can skate – doesn't get tired, and plays both ends of the rink. What else can you ask for?

MCCRIMMON Go back to the rationale for the Eichel trade in the first place – you end up with Eichel, Stephenson, Karlsson, Roy as your four centers. That is a really good way to run your hockey team; it gives you the ability to match up however you want, or not worry about matchups. We had good centermen prior to trading for Jack, and those three I just mentioned are really good NHL

CASSIDY Marchessault is competitive at practice, at games, and in the locker room. He came through in key situations, and he's been doing that here for years. I'm new, so I saw it firsthand this year. He can get emotional, which I think can detract from what he does. He gets caught up, like coaches do sometimes with officials' calls, more than most.

He's very vocal in every situation, no matter what, if he's playing good, bad, or indifferent. Good team guy who cares about his teammates. He is really good on the walls and doesn't get enough credit for that, considering his smaller body. He can be physical if he needs to. There were some games where he was hitting their biggest guys out there. Especially in the playoffs, that happens. Guys step up a little more in that area, and he certainly does.

The biggest challenge is managing his emotions to use them in the right way, because he can also get himself off his own game because of those emotions. Sometimes his greatest strength can also work against him. There are a lot of players like that. Brad Marchand, he's one. That's one that you just have to manage. Don't get too far across the line, but let him be himself.

MARCHESSAULT Until this season, the best hockey I've played in my life was with Karly and Smitty. It took Jack and me a while to figure out how to play with one another. Karly is one of the best centers in the NHL. And Reilly has been one of the faces of our franchise – part of the leadership group since the start. It's the heart of our team those guys. They lead us in so many ways. Karly gets down when he doesn't produce. But he plays against the best on the other side every game, every shift. Reilly has scored some big goals for us. And he's always been calm and positive. He's one of the best pros in the NHL.

EICHEL I think our depth means just as much as the guys that might get paid more and might get more of the statistical recognition. You're not winning without those guys. Martinez, what did he have? He had about 150 more blocked shots than anyone in the NHL, and then the next guy was Brayden McNabb. To me, that says one thing – that those are selfless guys. That's what that is.

Even Pietrangelo, he's up there every year in blocked shots, and he plays in every situation.

Keegan Kolesar, Nicolas Roy – you don't win without those guys. I don't think we even come close to doing what we did without them. For periods of the playoffs, our fourth line was playing against the other team's top line. It is truly a team effort.

JOHN STEVENS I'll be very candid and honest: This group of defensemen is the best group I've ever had to work with – and not just because of the players. It's the people that they are. What's interesting for me, I had McNabb and Marty as kids in LA. It was interesting for me to come around this time and see these guys as established veteran players who were really important veteran players on the back end.

Nabber and Theo are such different players that they complement each other so well. Nabber gives you size, and people who don't know him

OPPOSITE
Logan Thompson's March 23 win gave Vegas four straight victories with four different goaltenders, an NHL first.

ABOVE
Brayden McNabb played all 82 games in the regular season, and his +17 rating was his best since the team's inaugural season.

THE FORCE LINE

Lines get mixed and matched throughout a season based on production, chemistry, and health. Spending an extended period of time with the same linemates doesn't happen often.

The unit of Nicolas Roy, William Carrier, and Keegan Kolesar had the benefit of all three factors that go into keeping a line together. The trio earned the start in the majority of games in the playoffs, as Bruce Cassidy opted to use their speed and physicality to set the tone for his Golden Knights en route to the Stanley Cup.

"I would say that the building of the fourth line was important for our team and our group," Cassidy said. "I think they really helped identify how we wanted to play."

Energy and pace weren't the only dishes the Roy-Carrier-Kolesar line brought to the potluck. The line combined for 22 points (7 goals, 15 assists) during the run, including Carrier's game-deciding goal in Game 6 of

the Western Conference Final and Roy's game-winning goal in Game 2 of the Stanley Cup Final.

"I've got to give credit to Roy and Kolesar," Carrier said. "They're both not fourth-liners –

they could be third-liners with any other team, right? We could run that fourth line as a third line in any other team. So, credit to them, and they all had pretty good years offensively."

---

don't understand how intelligent he is as a hockey player – just how well he reads the game and sees the game, and what a good person he is. I thought Theo's best hockey was the end of the Dallas series and in the Final. Shea is elite. He can do things no one else can do.

Marty's just one of those guys. Marty was a third-pairing guy in LA on both Cup teams. And now he's playing with Petro. He's got the toughest matchup every night, trying to shut down the McDavids of the world, and just did an incredible job. There were a few times this year when Marty and Petro weren't in practice, and practices weren't as good – their leadership, the way they approach the game every day, their preparation level, how they helped get the room ready in their own way: relaxed, but ready and enjoying the game.

PIETRANGELO You can call Hague and Whitecloud a third pairing, but on any other team, they are in the top four – big and mobile and smart. And now they're experienced. They take a lot of hard

minutes off my back. We can put them out against anyone.

STONE I think our system, our defense, and the way the forwards committed to defense allowed our goalies to just make the saves. Yeah, we had some miraculous saves when we needed them at times. But if you let your goalie play, you know, with the talent that we have, they'll produce for us. The five guys that played, whether it was Logan Thompson to start, and then Adin Hill kind of took the reins a little bit. And then he got hurt. And Laurent Brossoit was playing great. He got hurt. So we needed some insurance. Jiri Patera came up and chipped in. And when we added Jonathan Quick, I think it added good, veteran leadership for those guys, too. Obviously, he didn't play games in the playoffs, but I'm sure if you ask those guys, he's helped them in their careers about being a great pro.

MCNABB Adin's got a lot of skill. I don't know how you define skill in a goalie or how that works. But he is a lot more than size – he handles the puck.

HOMEGROWN DEFENSEMEN

With six years of development and preparation under their belts, Nicolas Hague and Zach Whitecloud cemented themselves as a consistent, steady, homegrown defensive pair for the Vegas Golden Knights during the team's run to the Stanley Cup.

Hague was the fourth draft pick in franchise history as the team selected him 34th overall in the 2017 draft. Whitecloud was undrafted but signed as a college free agent after two seasons at Bemidji State University.

The duo formed a bond over the years as they skated together at Development Camps and Rookie Camps, tasted the NHL in preseason appearances, and paid their dues in the American Hockey League. Hague and Whitecloud became NHL regulars in the 2020-21 season and helped the Golden Knights reach the Western Conference Final.

Hague and Whitecloud are a success story of the organization's ability to identify

amateur talent, groom players to play in the NHL level, and fit those players into a system they can thrive in.

"I handed the Cup to Haguer. He and I have been partners for so long," Whitecloud said after winning the Stanley Cup. "It was cool to be able to hand it to him. I'm proud of the road we took to get here with this team and this organization."

Actually, he had times at the start of the year where he'd get himself in trouble handling the puck. He calmed it down a bit, which helped him and made him very good. But as a goalie, I don't know if he's just big, things just hit him. All I know is, he can stop the puck, and he can stop it well.

STEVENS If you look at the Winnipeg and Edmonton series, both were extremely physical. Nic Hague and Keegan Kolesar totally understand the flow of the game, the game within the game. There were times maybe we were up big in a game and somebody wants to get something going, they would just skate away. Other times, if anybody ever took advantage of a teammate, they'd be there to clean it up.

I think when teams know that you have guys like that on the other side, we don't need the referee to keep the peace. We can take care of our own backyard with guys like Kolesar and Brett Howden and Hague. Hague got in the face of a lot of people in the playoffs. The only one who would fight him

was Darnell Nurse. No one else was interested. He's become a force in that regard – not many guys in the league like him.

CARRIER In Boston, Bruce always had a great team and a solid defensive team. He didn't really tell us any role he wanted us to play, but he did say at the beginning of the year that he wanted to roll four lines, and he wanted us to play big minutes, so be ready. And that's another part of having a good year – our minutes were up a lot, every night, three or four minutes extra, starting every period, controlling the momentum of the game.

A lot of coaches say that when you meet them: "Oh, I'm gonna play my fourth line a lot," but they actually don't. Not as much as Bruce played us, and obviously, us playing well kind of forced him to play us even more. Nic Roy isn't a fourth-line center. He's so smart, and he can make plays. And Koley and I know our jobs. We can hit, and we can get to the net. Bruce made us feel important, and he stuck with us all season.

SHARING THE
SMYTHE

BY JONATHAN MARCHESSAULT

The Conn Smythe is kind of a funny trophy to win. It's great, but how do you look at a team like ours and pick out one person? The whole reason we won was our depth. They could have announced four or five different names for that award, and nobody would have been surprised.

I have been in Vegas from the beginning, and I remember, during those early days, thinking that people didn't give us enough credit for the talent in the room. We didn't know what to expect either, but once we got on the ice together, we had some really good players, as we showed.

But this team – this was the most talented group we've had, or I've ever been around. I guess that's obvious when you win the Stanley Cup – and win it convincingly, like we did. But it's true, and you can go down the roster and see why.

Start with Jack. I told him on the ice that he got me the Conn Smythe, and I stand by that. He can do so much on the ice, and he can almost make it look easy. It starts with his stride and how he covers so much ice so quickly. But he can pass, he can shoot, he can skate, he can defend – there really isn't anything he can't do.

I think I'm a pretty good player. I'm sure the other guys on the team will tell you that I'm a confident person. And I can play with good players, but I think I'm more of a complementary player. Guys like Jack – they just make everyone around them so much better.

Stoney is the same way. He just elevates the group. But he does it in a different way than Jack. Where Jack flies around the ice and you are in awe of his skill, Stoney creates time and space with his smarts. And what a leader. After what he did in Game 5, he could have easily won the Conn Smythe.

I can't go too far without mentioning my brothers, Smitty and Karly. Obviously, those guys are part of why I say the first team was more talented than people gave us credit for. They can do absolutely anything you want them to on the ice. First power play? First forwards on the PK? Score a big goal,

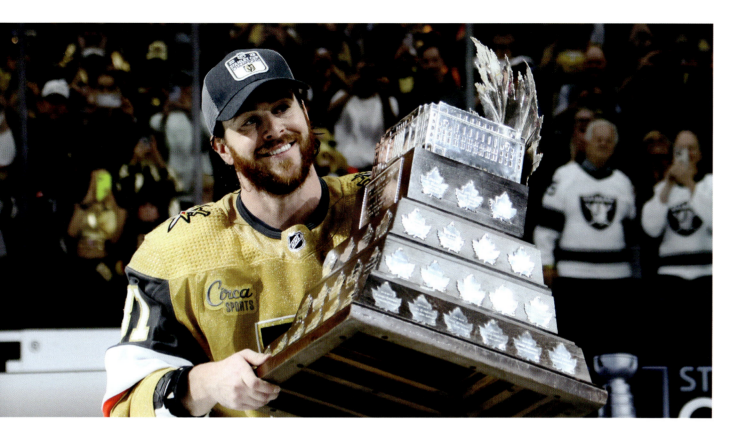

or block a shot? Those guys are complete hockey players. I'm so honored that people connect me with them. The name Misfits means a lot to me, and winning a championship together made it even sweeter.

I guess you can tell I'm a forward when I haven't mentioned a goalie or a defenseman yet. Adin was a rock for us in the playoffs, just as all our goalies were all year. Talk about another great Conn Smythe guy.

And our defense was probably the strength of our team. A guy like Petro amazes me, how he can do everything and do it all so well. He's strong, he's big, he's skilled – no wonder you look up at the end of the night and he's got a couple points, six blocked shots and a +3. And he plays half the game!

Shea is more of the flashy type, with his skating and his moves. If you made me play defense, that's the kind of stuff I would hope I could do.

I could keep going and probably name everybody on the roster. That's what I mean about being

surrounded by more talent than ever before. The true sign of our depth was probably how much our third pair or fourth line meant to us.

Haguer and Whitey really seemed to come into their own this spring. That night I had a hat trick in Edmonton, they were out there defending [Connor] McDavid and [Leon] Draisaitl in a six-on-five. There isn't another so-called third pair in the league that can do that.

The next series, we probably played our best game of the year – if not in franchise history – in Game 6 at Dallas. It was Roy-Kolesar-Carrier who led the way for us that night.

I guess I'm glad I didn't have to vote on the Conn Smythe. But I'm sure glad I got to share a room with these guys.

THE
ROOM

While talent can make a team a contender, Vegas Golden Knights players consistently point to an intangible when asked about their success in 2022-23: "It was fun to come to the rink every day."

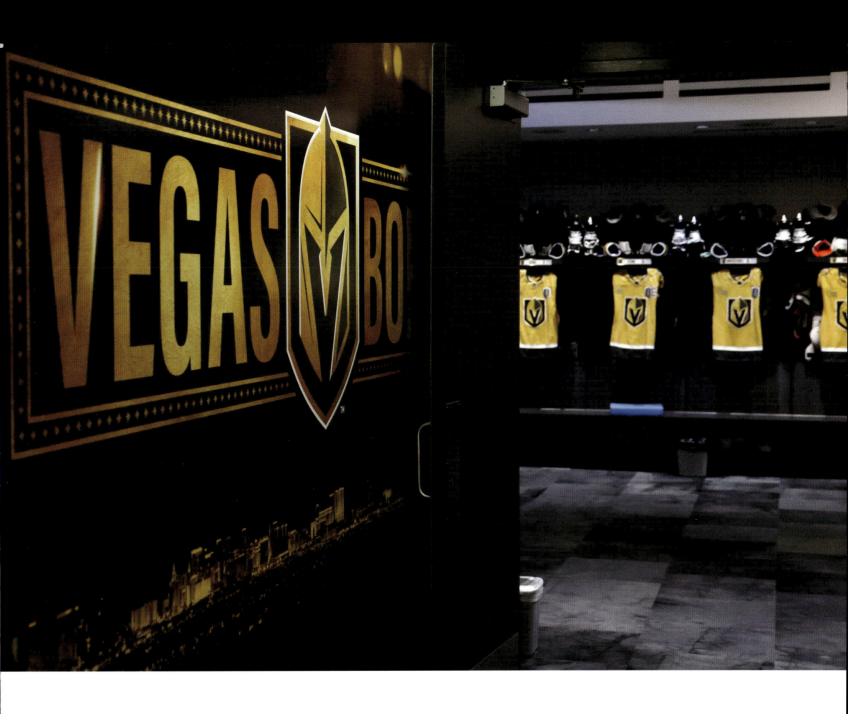

Four walls, benches, some stalls with hooks. That's a dressing room. But like a house becomes a home when you fill it with a family, a dressing room gains its soul when emptiness gives way to laughter, teasing, horseplay, and camaraderie.

The room, as players call it, becomes the wellspring of an organization. What happens in the dressing room determines where a team goes.

Good or bad.

+ + + + + +

BILL FOLEY With the current group we have, we went back to the way we were the first couple of years. The locker room was so animated, and the players were so supportive of one another in those first couple of years. They had been most of the

way through. In a few of those years, maybe our locker room wasn't what I would have liked to have seen.

I really honestly thought, beginning in the fall, with hiring Butch Cassidy and the players coming back healthy, that we were a team again. They liked each other. They enjoyed being around each other. We have as good a locker room as there is in the NHL right now.

JONATHAN MARCHESSAULT Our room was laid out perfect. Obviously, you always chit-chat with the guys next to you, but you always have Kolesar, Stephenson, and Eichel as the top three disturbers.

Well, we have a lot of rankings. We have the top three disturbers – I think Stevie was number one, Keegan was two, and Jack was three. They always say stuff to get me going. After I start chirping guys,

"VEGAS BORN" and the city skyline adorn the wall at the entrance to the Golden Knights' locker room at T-Mobile Arena.

No matter how competitive pregame soccer matches got – and they required a referee, William Carrier – they served as a unifying force.

and after everybody starts laughing, it's always the same jokes that come back around. It was just so much fun, to be honest.

On the plane, we have our card game, and honestly, it was too fun. It was so fun because it was always me and Jack across from Phil, and we would tease each other the whole time. I've never seen anything like it. Phil was just a character – there's nothing like that in the world. He's just so fun to be with and around, and Jack has a similar personality to me. He likes to always mess around, have fun, laugh, and say stupid stuff every day. It was just a good combo.

McNabb, he's sneaky – really funny as well. I don't know – it was just so much fun this year. Our card table was unbelievable.

RYAN CRAIG I want to give the returning guys credit because they were going to make sure our room wasn't an issue again. The leadership group that was returning was going to do that. The guys that we did add had some personalities. Right – Phil Kessel? It's our eighth game – the Ironman game – in San Jose. Kessel scores in that game, and you can see the bench – it's a different reaction. You can see the picture afterwards, the joy in everybody, and then it builds.

AROUND THE ROOM

Team chemistry is an abstract concept. The way players complement each other's style of play on the ice can differ from skater to skater.

The Vegas Golden Knights found the winning formula on the ice, but it was the chemistry forged off the ice that produced a cohesive band of brothers who were prepared to do anything for the team.

Let's take a lap around the locker room for an off-ice scouting report on each stall's occupant.

LEFT

KEEGAN KOLESAR: Volume increases as his teammates stir the pot. Calls every teammate "my bro!"

CHANDLER STEPHENSON: Infectious laugh. If he's laughing at a story, you know the whole group is laughing too.

BRETT HOWDEN: After complimenting a teammate, typically checks with Amadio for what he has planned for the rest of the day.

NICOLAS ROY: If not chatting with Carrier in French, he's smiling while Marchessault tells a story.

MICHAEL AMADIO: Usually quiet, but hilarious when he speaks up.

WILLIAM CARRIER: Waiting for a teammate to tell him an appliance isn't working at home and thinking of how he'll fix it. If there are no work orders, he's hustling to get out on the lake after practice.

PAUL COTTER: Probably getting an earful from his teammates about his shootout moves. When Cotter has the floor, you know some laughs are coming.

MIDDLE

ADIN HILL: Good luck finding Hill without a smile on his face, especially when the chirps are flying.

ZACH WHITECLOUD: Thoughtful guy who will probably compliment your outfit. Usually laughing at whatever rant Martinez is on.

ALEC MARTINEZ: Pick a topic and bring it up. He's got an opinion and a story that is guaranteed to leave you laughing.

NICOLAS HAGUE: Probably asked Martinez a question that sparked the day's conversation.

BRAYDEN MCNABB: Loves the action going on around the room and gets his quiet jabs in when the time is right and others are unsuspecting.

SHEA THEODORE: Loves bringing up funny YouTube videos or social media clips. Always quoting *The Office* and relating the show to everyday life.

ALEX PIETRANGELO: Ear to the ground, waiting for the right time to add a zinger or correct someone's recollection of a story.

BEN HUTTON: Usually hyping up his teammates for something cool they did on the ice. Especially loves seeing his fellow defensemen score during practice.

JONATHAN QUICK: Meshed seamlessly with his new team. Became a mentor for the other goalies.

RIGHT

LAURENT BROSSOIT: Quietly goes about his business and loves talking shop with his fellow goaltenders.

TEDDY BLUEGER: Will talk to anyone about anything and can do it in almost any language.

IVAN BARBASHEV: Not the loudest guy in the room, but loves seeing others stir the pot and get on each other's case.

WILLIAM KARLSSON: Loves to add "oohs" and "ahhs" to stories being told or conversations being had.

PHIL KESSEL: If someone is chirping Kessel – and a teammate usually is – they'd better be ready to take a chirp back. Always laughing with his stall mates about something.

JACK EICHEL: Usually the one chirping Kessel.

MARK STONE: Leader by example, but always has time for a laugh.

JONATHAN MARCHESSAULT: Probably the voice you heard a step or two before you walked into the room. He can hold a conversation with anyone, whether they're next to him or across the room.

REILLY SMITH: A quiet leader. Always taking the temperature of the room and offering whatever the group needs.

I thought our guys really stood up for each other through the year – they came up in big games. It wasn't fake. When we went into Boston, the guys played that hard and were happy for Bruce. It wasn't fake when we went into Buffalo and Jack Eichel scored the hat trick, and our guys couldn't be happier.

BRUCE CASSIDY We had the stuff around Phil Kessel at the start of the year. His streak helped our guys come together a little bit. It was early in the year, when he was going for the record. I thought that helped us, to have a different goal besides just playing a team game. We were pulling for a teammate that was popular.

WILLIAM KARLSSON We had some fun right off the start – started feeling good about one another. Phil was chasing the Ironman record, and we were getting to know him. It was a common goal and something to get behind. We won in San Jose, and his dad was around that night. It gave us a feeling of accomplishing something early on. It was his record, but we all helped get the win. We never really let that positive feeling go away.

JACK EICHEL Phil meant so much to our team. You need characters in your room, you need personalities, you need people that keep it light when maybe things aren't going well. And Phil brings all that, but he also brings experience. He's played

OPPOSITE
Alec Martinez (left) and Shea Theodore shared a laugh the morning of Game 6 in Dallas.

ABOVE
Vegas hit the halfway mark on a three-game winning streak thanks to this 5–2 victory against Pittsburgh.

MEET WILLIAM CARRIER

There are very few stats that aren't tracked in today's NHL. If you dig deep enough online, you can find just about any hockey data you're looking for.

William Carrier would be among the league leaders in a number of categories the statisticians couldn't hope to record. If fish caught, homes built, garages repaired, lighting fixtures installed, and tires changed were stats that someone kept track of, Carrier would clean up at the NHL Awards.

If trips to the Marchessaults' house to fix or build something were goals, Carrier would be a perennial Rocket Richard Trophy winner.

He's the first person a teammate calls when an appliance isn't working at home. Rather than giving a plumber, electrician, or for-hire handyman a few hundred dollars, teammates pay Carrier for his services in tape-to-tape passes and bottles of wine.

When he's not at the rink, helping a teammate, or being a family man at home, Carrier has bait on his hook and a line in the water. Whether it's a day trip to Lake Mead, a summer voyage to Alaska in search of halibut, or hopping from lake to lake in Quebec in the offseason, you'll find the veteran forward reeling in a fish before you'll find him scrolling through social media.

so long in this league. He's obviously won twice. He's been on different teams. He's been in different markets, different cities. I think the element of experience with Phil was really great for our team.

The way that his personality is, he's able to bring guys together and keep things light. I just thought from the minute he came in in training camp, he was so special to our group and what he meant to the locker room – just how much he cared about guys and how much guys cared about him.

Through the playoffs, he ended up not playing, but it never changed his mood, never changed the way he approached it. He'd come to the rink every day, a smile on his face. I really enjoy seeing him. I enjoy sitting next to him. He kept it light for me all year before games. I'm just so glad to have gotten the opportunity to play with him and develop a friendship.

ADIN HILL It was just a true team. Off the ice too, we're all best friends, all hanging out, laughing every day. Coming to the rink was just awesome. You enjoyed your time at the rink – you almost didn't want to leave.

We just had a good culture, good atmosphere. Practices were fun, as you could probably see from the stands – all hooting and hollering the whole practice. I think Marchy kind of got that going. It is just a fun team to be around. And the energy flows throughout the team. Everybody loves everyone. I think that was just kind of the perfect setup for us leading into the playoffs.

ALEC MARTINEZ I hate using this word, because it's so cliché, but the camaraderie – the feeling that you get when you go to the rink. The feeling when you're comfortable and you feel like you're amongst your people. It's a sense of comfort.

There are a lot of things that can bring a group of people together, and sports is up there on the list. It's not just the team, but look at T-Mobile Arena: Every fan in that building for Game 5, all on the same page, all happy, and everyone is feeling it together.

Although this would have been really difficult for me to come around to if we hadn't won, this might go down as one of my most fun years I've ever had, even if we didn't win. I've been fortunate to be a part of – not just in pro hockey, but when I was in Juniors, we won the USHL. I played on some really good teams at Miami, and we won a league championship. It's a certain feeling in the room, and I always felt inside that we had the right group to get

William Karlsson ended every warmup skate with a word and a handshake with Raul Dorantes, the team's manual therapist.

it done. It takes a lot more than that, but that feeling in the room with people who genuinely care about each other is special.

There are a lot of things at play. I think the circumstances helped make a difference – the city that we're in, the original Misfits, and to see those guys be able to do it. It's a hard question, but it's more of a feeling than something that I can describe.

WILLIAM KARLSSON It felt like year one again. We really loved one another on this team. And that kept growing throughout the year. We used the outside gossip as fuel. And we pulled together. It made us invincible again.

JONATHAN MARCHESSAULT We needed to get back to our attitude in the first season in Vegas. And we did. Guys were pissed off that we missed the playoffs the year before. And we added a few guys – new coaches and Phil Kessel.

All of a sudden, we're having fun again and sticking together. No cliques. A family. And we're good. What a team. So we started winning early, and it never really stopped. We had the one bad spot before the All-Star break. It came at the right time. But the way the guys came to camp and the wins early on, it set the tone for us.

EICHEL Everyone knows about the way things went my first year with Vegas and returning to Buffalo. That was a tough night for me, no doubt, and probably one of the toughest nights, if not the toughest night, in my career. There wasn't a need to say a whole lot – I think everyone in the group knew what that next game meant to me.

Having the guys all react the way that they did during the game, that just meant so much to me. Moments like that bring the group together. It felt like it was us, and we had so many people against us.

Hockey players are creatures of habit by nature. It's the best way to ensure peak performance during the grind of an 82-game schedule and a grueling Stanley Cup tournament.

Each player on the Vegas Golden Knights has little things he does during warm-ups that stick out from his teammates' habits. For starters, William Carrier always follows the starting goalie out to the ice and knocks the pucks from the edge of the bench to the playing surface. When he reaches the end of the pile, he takes one puck, puts it up on its edge, and leaves it there. It remains upright until Brayden McNabb grabs it a few players later and tosses it onto the ice.

Once the team is on the ice, Alec Martinez does his stretches in front of the Golden Knights bench and laughs with anyone who's around at funny signs in the crowd. Once everyone has taken a few laps around the ice, they gather in the corners and wait for Jonathan Marchessault to shoot a puck down to the other end of the ice. That's the signal that drills are starting.

Shea Theodore and William Karlsson always find a moment for their nightly tradition they've had for six seasons: As Karlsson stretches at one of the neutral zone faceoff dots, Theodore gives him a few light whacks with his hockey stick, shakes his hand, and gives him a pat on the head. Karlsson then skates over to the bench for his conversation and handshake with Raul Dorantes, the team's manual therapist.

Adin Hill's warm-up routine consists of taking some shots from his teammates, doing a few stretches in the neutral zone, and working on a couple of puck tricks to keep things loose. When he's in the zone, his teammates know it. Before Game 3 of the Western Conference Final, Jonathan Quick watched Hill for five minutes in warm-ups before he leaned over the bench and predicted a shutout against the Dallas Stars that night. Vegas won the game, 4–0, and Hill had a 34-save clean sheet.

Chandler Stephenson takes a look at the bench before he does his final zooms around the ice. If he's spotted someone on the team staff not paying attention, there's a good chance they're in for a snow shower from the speedy center. Nicolas Hague has been the unfortunate recipient of the blast of snow on occasion. He spends a few minutes

standing by the bench dousing himself, and sometimes a bystander, in water.

For a while during the 15-minute skate-around before puck drop, Mark Stone stands at the blueline and takes in what's happening around him. He delicately brushes snow from the blade of his stick as he watches teammates buzz around the ice. When he's finished soaking in the scene, he skates hard toward the net and goes about his business. Toward the end of warm-ups, Stone skates over to the bench and shakes hands with every VGK staffer before heading to the locker room. This is usually about when McNabb caps off his pregame routine with a few stick handles, a booming

slapshot, and a twirl of the stick before exiting.

Sometime after the majority of the players have left the ice, the shooting gallery opens. Alex Pietrangelo and Jonathan Marchessault feed each other passes and hammer them into the back of the net. Shea Theodore and Jack Eichel do the same when they're done. Eichel is usually the last to leave the ice, and does so with a puck in his hand destined to be tossed to a lucky fan.

About 20 minutes later, the Golden Knights return to the ice with game faces on and a victory to claim.

It was a lot easier for me because I looked around and I knew these guys had my back after knowing them for a year. I'd spent time with them and done more stuff away from the rink with them. It just felt different. I knew they were going to come out and perform, and then the whole group did. To be able to do that in Buffalo – get a win and a hat trick – it was an emotional night.

ADIN HILL It took us a while to kind of get our player-of-the-game thing going to start the year. We were just handing out pucks to start, but Eichel kept kind of being, like, 'I got something coming – I got something coming.' And we were waiting for it.

So he got the wig and the glasses. And you know what? It's perfect. Because we're in Vegas. Makes sense. Just kind of goes to the player that we felt had the biggest game. I don't really know if there's a definition for it, whether it's MVP or the biggest kind of game changer. Maybe you made a hit that changed the course of the whole game, right? Something like that.

So whoever got it last picks the most valuable player of the game. It's a fun vibe in the locker room, especially when it's a wig like that too. Because you see each guy kind of put it on and everyone looks a little different in it. It keeps it light.

EICHEL We wanted to switch it up. I asked Mark Stone what he thought we could get – a jacket made that we could put on after the game and have someone put Vegas stuff on the jacket. Then, I asked him about the Elvis wig, and he said that was great.

I ordered it on Amazon, and it came in. I think the wig was around $30 and the glasses were, like, $15. Perfect, we don't need anything fancy. The Elvis wig, it was cool.

It was something that for a majority of the season, no one really knew about, and then it came to light towards the end of the year. It was always funny – you'd see someone new put it on, and then we'd make a comment. Just more ways to bring the group together.

There was a stretch before the Elvis wig came in where we were just passing around a protective cup. It wasn't someone's jock that they were wearing, but we literally had a spare cup that we would pass out.

Obviously, you want to give something out, and you want that guy who was the player of the game to say something. It's a big tradition after a game – the postgame tradition. I don't remember the first time I had the wig, but obviously, it was cool. I took a lot of pride in it, and I'm happy it was received well, and the guys thought it was cool.

BRAYDEN MCNABB Our guys like to have fun. And our room is really fun. The Elvis wig was meaningful in a couple ways – seeing everyone put it on and how goofy we all looked in it. It's hard to be serious in that get-up.

OPPOSITE
Ivan Barbashev's three-point game in Game 3 at Dallas helped put Vegas one win away from the Stanley Cup Final.

ABOVE
William Karlsson (left) and Reilly Smith personified the loose mood that defined most of Vegas' game-day morning skates.

MADE OF IRON

Picture this: you've been the NHL's Ironman record holder for a week and a half. You're about to break your own record as you suit up for your 994th consecutive NHL game. Your name is Phil Kessel, and your Vegas Golden Knights are in Ottawa to face the Senators.

Looking back with laughter, Jonathan Marchessault shared the story on the popular *Spittin' Chiclets* podcast of a pregame mishap that almost put Kessel's Ironman streak into jeopardy.

Warm-ups were about 20 minutes away. The usual suspects were kicking a soccer ball around to loosen up before the game as they prepared for their second game of the road trip.

"Where's Marchy?" asked a few of the players.

It was past time for him to make his triumphant entry into the soccer game.

Marchessault walked by clutching his forehead. Players shouted to him to join their game. He removed his hand to reveal blood coming from an open cut that he had mysteriously obtained.

Meanwhile, hockey tape was used to lay out an outline of Marchessault's body, with the number 81 in the middle, on the changing room floor. The pregame excitement turned to confusion until his teammates heard an explanation.

While the rest of the team had been in the midst of pregame routines, Marchessault and Kessel had been firing each other up for the game with some playful chirping. There was no real argument or bad blood of any kind as the two came together with

laughter. They were on the same page about the exchange and, unfortunately, had the same exact thought at the same exact time.

Both players went to throw a fake headbutt at the same moment, and they ended up knocking heads. Kessel received what Marchessault described as a "little mosquito bite" on his forehead, while Marchessault had to see the trainer to get stitched up before warm-ups.

"Everyone was dying, laughing, coming to see me get stitches before the game," Marchessault said. "That trip got our team bonding really going. It was just so funny."

Ironman took on a new meaning that night for Kessel.

But it was interesting to see who guys picked. It was not always the guy who had the most points in a game. If a guy had a big hit and changed the game, or blocked a shot at a key moment, he ended up in the wig. We valued things that led to wins. Sure, goals are part of that. But all the little things that teammates notice when winning is the focus, they were key to who got picked on a lot of nights. And it was a great feeling to pull that wig on and wear those shades.

MARTINEZ We block more shots than any other team, and it says so much about our group. Selfless. Because you have to be if you want to win – it's as simple as that. Growing up, it wasn't really, like, an emphasis or anything. Maybe it's a product of the game changing, equipment getting slightly better, or a little bit of both.

I've talked to a few guys about this. It's funny because it's such a false sense of security, having all that gear on, because at the end of the day, it's just plastic. If that puck were coming at me, sitting here right now, I'd be jumping through the window behind me to get out of the way before I blocked it.

But when you put on a few pieces of plastic, then things change and you're willing to just step right in front of it.

The short answer is, you just have to do that stuff in order to win. It shows that there's two kinds of people, or two kinds of players in the league – someone that has the talent and can play the game well, and then there are the people that are in the league because they're willing to do things that others aren't. Maybe the third one is a combination of both. We have a lot of those third-combination guys.

EICHEL I love the place and I love the organization. I mean, I have a VGK logo tattooed on my leg now. What Kelly, George, and Bill mean to me for bringing me in and giving me the opportunity. What the guys in the room mean to me.

I was down and out. I wasn't even playing hockey. I never looked at it like I'm a Misfit 2.0, because obviously, these got taken in the Expansion Draft, but there are a lot of guys in that room that got the short end of the stick in a situation, or more

ABOARD AIR VGK

In each of the sections on the Vegas Golden Knights' team plane, you can find members of the team and staff doing a variety of things to pass the time at 35,000 feet.

At the front of the plane, you'll find team management and the coaching staff. They'll keep their suits on for the most part, depending on the length of the flight. Maybe a few will shed their jacket and just wear their dress shirt. A bulk of the voyage is spent watching film, be it from the game before, the next opponent's most recent game, or a movie they've had downloaded that it's finally time to enjoy.

Walk back a few rows, and you'll find some veterans playing cards or chatting while the plane makes its way around the continent. The suits they wore on the plane are neatly hung up and the sweatshirts and gym shorts they packed in their bags are being worn to ensure comfort during the flight.

Some players will be getting some sleep or just kicking back and watching a season of a show on their iPad. When you walk past Zach Whitecloud's seat, he'll be watching *Trailer Park Boys*. Nicolas Hague is watching a Marvel movie with Keegan Kolesar. Shea Theodore is laughing at the latest YouTube video a buddy had sent him.

When you get to the middle of the plane, there's a voice that echoes louder than the plane's engines. It's Jonathan Marchessault's. He's sitting with Brayden McNabb, Jack Eichel, and Phil Kessel at one of the card tables. There's hooting and hollering about the last hand and some chirps flying in an attempt to get whoever's winning off his game.

As you get toward the back, you'll find other players taking a nap, looking out the window, or bingeing something on Netflix or Hulu. Behind them, the rest of the team staff is catching up on sleep, preparing notes for

the next broadcast, and cooking up social media posts.

The plane begins its descent into the next city as the suits go back on, devices are put away, and the entire travel party's eyes become fixed on the challenge ahead.

---

than one situation. A lot of teams decided that they didn't want you.

I can appreciate the organization that brings you in. That's the feeling that you get, and that's why it works. I think everyone takes a lot of pride in being a part of it.

WILLIAM CARRIER One night, I might go out with Petro and Phil and Marty for a nice dinner. But the day after, I'm with the younger guys, like Kolesar and Roy, for sushi. I think we had a group of guys that really mixed together. We had chemistry, obviously, with lines, like the Misfits and guys like that, but at the end of the day, everyone was kind of matching together. It felt like the first year, where guys knew that business is on the ice and worked hard.

Guys hate losing and they want to win, but they still made sure we had fun. And it's tough to balance it. Because you do want to have fun – you do want to be loose, but not too loose. The older guys like Marty and Petro, especially Phil, they're always

setting stuff up on a day off – team dinners and stuff. Kind of brings everyone out, and once you've tasted that with the group of guys, you want it more and more.

CRAIG It was all real, and it was genuine. I think that's why there was belief in our team. With our depth and how much guys believed in each other, we could do something special. I don't want to say destiny, but we were able to find ways to come together as a team. It wasn't going to be an individual that was going to pull us out of anything, any hole we were in. It was going to be the team.

MARK STONE Where else do you get to go to work with 25 of your best friends? I didn't want to miss this. I wanted to get back on the team to be part of it. I missed them and playing with them so much. Watching is so hard. This was just such a fun team to be around and to play with. It's the best team experience I've ever been a part of.

OPPOSITE
Jonathan Marchessault (left) and Adin Hill embraced in the locker room after the Game 4 win in Florida.

THE ODD
COUPLE

BY PAUL COTTER

I really wasn't expecting to write an essay for this Stanley Cup championship book. Once I left Vegas for the summer, I figured I could golf and think about what to do on my day with the Cup.

Look at the other guys who were asked to contribute! Jack, Stoney, Marchy – no way they ask the rookie to help out.

Well, in fairness, they didn't just ask for me; they asked for me and Phil Kessel to do something together. I said sure. Phil said something along the lines of "Who the heck wants to hear what I have to say, eh?"

So, as Phil's designated literary agent, I'm here to announce that he's turning this one down. He's probably turned down as many media opportunities in a row as he has played regular-season games.

But I guess they wanted the two of us to do this for a reason. Apparently, as the rest of the guys got interviewed for this book, they kept mentioning

"Phil and Paul." Not sure why us – maybe they're jealous of the way we tape our sticks.

I guess they also think we kept things loose and light in the room. I'm not exactly sure what Phil and I had to do with that, but I can tell you it was a great group to play hockey with. We had fun all the time – during practice, on the road, in the lounge, in the weight room. (Maybe not Phil in the weight room.)

Having such a great room helped keep Phil's and my spirits up when we weren't in the playoff lineup. He, of course, played every regular-season game, as he always has. I played most of them in my first full NHL season. We both wanted to be in the lineup – don't get me wrong – but I was still smiling: I was in the NHL. Heck, Phil was still smiling, and he's always been in the NHL.

Phil's and my personalities seemed to mesh. I think it's safe to say we both take hockey very seriously, but we don't take ourselves too seriously.

Maybe the two of us got along because everybody else always had a jab to throw our way. We like to think we can both answer pretty well, which might be why they kept coming.

Keeping the room light isn't something we planned or put any thought into. We were just who we are, and people seemed to like it. It was still

fun to come to the rink every day, and we looked forward to it.

Though it's true that Phil threatened the guys that they needed to win Game 5, because there was no way in hell he was getting back on that plane to Florida.

He was probably scared to lose to me in poker.

THE
SEASON

The Vegas Golden Knights' regular season had ups and downs as they battled injuries but always seemed to overcome them. A brilliant stretch run set them up for postseason success.

The NHL's 82-game regular season is the six-month prologue that lays the foundation for postseason glory.

The 2022–23 Golden Knights broke out winning 13 of their first 15 games, propelling them to a Western Conference–best 51-win season.

The signposts along this Vegas hockey odyssey were significant:

- Bruce Cassidy and Jack Eichel enjoyed triumphant returns to their old NHL towns.

- Chandler Stephenson and Logan Thompson became NHL All-Stars.

- The team struggled through a slump heading into the All-Star break.

- Mark Stone required a second back surgery within a year which cost him 39 regular season games.

- Injuries to the blueline pushed Shea Theodore out of the lineup for 27 games and Zach Whitecloud for 23 games. A family medical issue forced Alex Pietrangelo to leave the team for nine games.

- Various ailments up front resulted in lengthy absences including Brett Howden missing 28 games, Will Carrier 28 games and Nic Roy 17 games.

- Goaltending was a strength for the Golden Knights all season despite having to use five different goalies.

- A 22-8-2 mark versus the Eastern Conference was a preview to Vegas being elite no matter the opposition.

- A Fathers' Trip brought the best out of the team.

- A roaring stretch run held off the Oilers, Kings, Kraken, Avalanche and Stars to clinch the division and the conference.

- A fantastic start and equally impressive finish coincided with health. When the full lineup was together, the Golden Knights were the NHL's best team.

Brett Howden was limited to 54 games due to injury but played 33 of the final 34, setting himself up for an impressive playoff performance.

+ + + + +

BRUCE CASSIDY It was important for me that we get off to a good start. Because you're a new coach, you've changed some of the ways the team is going to play. If you win, the players tend to be more receptive to it. That's fairly typical in any sport.

When you have a start like that, the players start believing that we're going to get back to where we were the first four years and not the last year. You're winning and finding ways to win. I don't think it was lucky.

We sat there and said, Logan Thompson isn't necessarily stealing games every night. Did Logan Thompson play well when given an opportunity? Absolutely. Different guys were scoring, so I thought that was important for our mentality. We're a team that is winning – the Knights are winning. It's not Jack Eichel or the goalie – it's the team.

MARK STONE In the previous season, we didn't have a good start. We had to fight hard to get back to where we wanted to be. We were number one

Michael Amadio (No. 22) scored on December 21 to start a three-game goal-scoring streak and a stretch in which he scored five times in six games.

OPPOSITE
The Golden Knight summoned the helmet prior to the team taking the ice each home game.

in the division for a lot of the season, but we had to fight hard to get there.

The way we started this year, I think we were 13–2. And if you look at 13–2, you probably think you could play .500 hockey the rest of the way and get in the playoffs. I think that helped when we went through tough patches in December, when we lost a few bodies. Then, in January, we lost a few more bodies and we were able to hang around a little bit above .500.

Once we got healthy after the All-Star break, we were still in a great position, we were still leading our division, we were still right where we wanted to be. That start allowed us to keep things rolling and tread water a little bit through the tough patches.

ALEX PIETRANGELO I missed nine games mid-season when my daughter got sick. It could have been a lot worse. She's doing a lot better, but there's still a long road. We know families who have gone through this, and it's taken a year for their kids to get where our daughter got in a few weeks.

At that point, I'm, like, "Jayne, if I'm going to take a whole year off, forget it – I'm not going back. I may never play again." I didn't even think about it. And all of a sudden, she gets better. She improved a lot in a short period of time, and I was able to return.

You learn a lot about your team going through something like that. The whole group was there for us – everybody texting and trying to help.

I think for me, especially from Kelly and George and Bill, I already respect them, but even more so because not once through that entire thing did they say to me, "Hey, what do you think time frame-wise?" Not a single question. It was, "You tell us when your family's ready, and we'll be ready to take you back. In the meantime, we'll handle things on

"NABBER, MY BRO!!!"

The Vegas Golden Knights creative minds got together and quickly whipped up a script after learning that rapper Lil Jon was up for doing a skit with the team. The piece was one in a series of humorous spots under the theme of "The Golden Age" that also included a *Dumb and Dumber* spoof with Bill Foley and a new team pet, Goldie the Goldfish.

The premise of this one: new "assistant coach" Lil Jon was going to address the team and tell them to take more shots – a nod to the artist's hit "Shots" from 2009.

As lines were written, Eric Tosi, VGK's chief marketing officer, offered the idea:

"We should have Lil Jon call on specific players and see what we get from it!"

A fan since the 2017–18 inaugural season, Lil Jon knew many of the Golden Knights players by name. During the video shoot at City National Arena, he enthusiastically bellowed a line that stuck with the team all season long.

"Nabber, my bro!!!! Whatcha got?"

The line was recorded before the season just in front of staff, and the remaining scenes of the viral commercial were stitched together later with Vegas players. The editing process began, and, in early November, the video was released on the team's social media platforms.

As the views on the video multiplied, the line began to grow from a one-off piece of dialogue to an everyday quip in the Vegas

locker room. Even with noise-canceling headphones on during a team flight, one can hear Jonathan Marchessault shout, "Nabber, MY BRO!!!" during a card game.

It might not be the nickname McNabb would've picked, but he's not one to kill the fun.

---

our end." I think that showed my teammates a lot. And it showed me a lot, because it's not an easy thing to do, obviously.

GEORGE MCPHEE The only way to deal with players and operate your team is simple: There's a right way and a wrong way. There's nothing in between. So do it right. Every time. Every single thing. From the top down to the bottom up. Big or small. It has to be the right way. There is always a human element. This player and his family were in a very difficult place. Nothing else mattered besides getting their daughter healthy. We needed to support them to do whatever they needed to do.

PIETRANGELO It was kind of good timing hockey-wise. Obviously, I play a lot of minutes, so this meant new responsibilities for a lot of guys. It was actually weird, because I miss time, then I come back, and Shea Theodore and Zach Whitecloud get hurt.

It almost worked out – I don't want to say it's good that they got hurt, but the timing was OK, because imagine if all of us had been out at the same time? It would have been a tough situation.

As a group defensively, I was proud of our guys because I felt like everybody stepped up. And that played a big part for guys like Haguer and Whitey, the way they played in the playoffs, because they knew that they could play bigger minutes at a higher level.

KELLY MCCRIMMON Mark Stone got hurt again in January. The first thing you think is, what, exactly, happened, and how can we deal with it? You think about the player. And then, how was our team going to respond? We played our worst two games of the year, the next two – Saturday at home to LA, Monday at home to Dallas. And we lost six of seven going into the break.

The hope was Mark could rehab and return coming out of the break. You see it sometimes where teams consciously or subconsciously just wait until that guy gets back. Then it was evident that surgery was going to be required.

It at least gave us a week to get our heads around what this new version of ourselves was going to be. I think that allowed us to stop the spiral, and then we had six healthy D coming out of the break, and that helped us get going.

STONE I thought everything was going pretty smooth. Obviously, had the surgery last summer and was feeling great going into training camp. Feeling great throughout the season. The team was playing amazing. Now we were in first place in our division and our conference. Just loved everything that was happening.

It was January 12 against Florida, ironically. I went to make a play, and shooting pain went through my back again. I went to the locker room – didn't know what was next. I was crying. Thought maybe that was the end of the season, at least for me.

But I regrouped. It took me about two weeks to try and rehab – try and see if I could do something the rest of the season. I had another terrible incident

in the weight room that took me down again to my knees. So right then and there, I knew that I was probably going to have to go under the knife again.

I think if you ask any player who's been through long rehabs, there's some long days, tough days that it's hard to wake up and come to the rink. And then, ultimately, being able to come in and still be a part of the team and still do everything that I like to do with my teammates – that helps, right? When you come into the rink and the team is winning, and you get to spend time around your teammates, it makes it easier.

Whenever the team would go on the road, it was tougher for the guys rehabbing. And that's what I tried to do – still mingle with the team, try and go

As part of a tradition started this year, Three Stars honorees like Jack Eichel tossed autographed pillows shaped like poker chips into the crowd after home games.

THEME KNIGHTS

The Golden Knights hosted 10 theme games during the 2022-23 season. Each specialty game featured unique warm-up jerseys, themed in-arena elements, and charitable initiatives to benefit local nonprofit organizations through the VGK Foundation.

The promotional schedule began with Nevada Day on October 28. The Golden Knights celebrated the Silver State with a 4-0 victory against the Anaheim Ducks as Vegas wore its white uniforms for the annual Friday matinee.

On November 12, the organization saluted armed service members on Military Appreciation Knight by raising money for the Folded Flag Foundation, which serves Gold Star families. Later that month, the Golden Knights donned lavender warm-up sweaters for Hockey Fights Cancer Knight.

Hispanic Heritage Knight was celebrated on December 7 at T-Mobile Arena as the Golden Knights wore an alternate warm-up uniform inspired by the significance of the marigold flower in Hispanic cultures. Stephanie Suominen, who is of Colombian descent and a junior graphic designer for the Golden Knights, led the creation process for the jersey.

The Golden Knights teamed up with Swedish artist Mio Linzie to create the rainbow warm-up jerseys the team wore on PRIDE

Knight on January 5. The sweaters and rainbow-taped sticks were auctioned off to benefit the Henderson Equality Center.

On January 21, the Golden Knights went all out for Lunar New Year Knight with red warm-up jerseys, which had the team's name and players' names written in Chinese. The Year of the Rabbit was rung in properly as Vegas defeated Washington, 6-2.

Jalen Jones, motion graphics designer for the Golden Knights, worked with Keegan Kolesar to design the specialty warm-up

jerseys for Black History Month Knight on February 16. The team then celebrated Women's History Month for the first time as Vegas used the game to benefit the Shade Tree, an organization that shelters Las Vegas women and their children.

After celebrating St. Patrick's Day midway through March, the Golden Knights closed out their promotional schedule with Donate Life Knight on April 6. Through the team's partnership with the Nevada Donor Network, the game raised awareness for organ-donation sign-ups in Nevada.

---

to a few meetings when you could. That's why this team, this sport, is so special. You always can feel a part of it.

BRAYDEN MCNABB We lost six of seven going into the All-Star break. We had our trip through New York, and we didn't win a game. We should have won in New Jersey, but the puck went off my leg in the last minute and then we lost in overtime. That one was tough.

I feel like no matter what team you are, you're going to have struggles. And if you don't, you're probably going to have struggles at the wrong time of year. It's good to face adversity. And you do want to face

it early on or midway through the year – not late in the season or in playoffs.

I remember Butch coming in and having a little bit of an emotional speech and just saying, "Enjoy your break – we'll turn things around. We're playing the right way, but we're not getting rewarded." And that's the biggest thing: If you're playing the right way but you're not getting rewarded, you know things are going to turn around. And they did. We came back and played awesome after the break.

JOHN STEVENS I remember vividly going into the office. We sat down as a staff – George and Kelly came down. And it was tight. We were as close

REVERSE RETRO 2023

Hit the lights.

The Vegas Golden Knights and Adidas collaborated on one of the most unique uniforms in the history of sports in 2022–23 during the NHL's Reverse Retro initiative.

Inspired by the neon lights so deeply associated with Las Vegas, the Golden Knights became the first team in professional sports to have glow-in-the-dark elements on their one-of-a-kind jersey. With the lights on, the black jersey features the word *Vegas* displayed diagonally in the iconic font of the Excalibur Hotel & Casino. It was the first time the team had deviated from its primary or secondary logo on a uniform and instead bore the name of its city across the chest.

When the lights go out, the letters on the front come to life with a green glow that shines as bright as the city it represents. The numbers on the sleeves and back react to ultraviolet light to shine with a blue-purple hue.

"To be able to dive into our city's history and pull elements from iconic '90s hotels and connect it with our VGK brand was an amazing opportunity," said Brady Hackmeister, creative director for the Golden Knights. "We are always striving to be innovative while staying authentic to who we are. We really pushed Adidas to bring the

glow elements to life. The first time the guys walked the tunnel was incredible. Seeing *Vegas* shining, almost floating toward the ice, was surreal and the culmination of months of hard work by so many people."

The jersey was a hot seller as fans lined up outside City National Arena before the sun rose on the day the sweater went on sale. Hats, jackets, shirts, pucks, and all kinds of apparel flew off the shelves and became regulars in the gear rotation of Golden Knights supporters.

Vegas wore the specialty uniform on eight occasions – all at home – and produced some magic moments on the ice. The second

time the team wore the Reverse Retro kits, Jonathan Marchessault delivered an overtime winner against the Philadelphia Flyers as he flew past the defense to tuck a backhand shot into the cage. On New Year's Eve, Nicolas Hague pounded a puck into the cage to defeat the Nashville Predators in overtime, 54, with the diagonal *Vegas* across his chest.

While the uniform was retired with the end of the 2022–23 Reverse Retro initiative, the innovative jersey will remain a favorite for Golden Knights players and fans alike.

OPPOSITE
The glow-in-the-dark elements in the Reverse Retro jerseys were the first of their kind in pro sports.

to winning the division, winning the conference, as we were to being out of the playoffs. It was that close.

Something clicked, and we woke up and got going. We understood how hard it was going to be. I think there was a really good understanding, from that point on coming out of the break, that if we were playing the game the right way, if we were committed to the structure we wanted to play with, we could play with anybody. And we certainly proved it.

RYAN CRAIG We had had success before that stretch where we went 1–5–2, so we had seen

what good hockey was. It just seemed like we were spinning our tires a little bit and everybody was probably ready for a break. That break came at the right time for us, and our record speaks for itself afterwards.

I think the guys self-evaluated a little bit, looked at the opportunity in front of us. They didn't want to waste it, because at that point, I think we were hovering around the playoff picture. Our division was that tight, where we were anywhere from first to a wild card team, or right around there.

MCCRIMMON I thought our first game in Nashville after the break was the biggest game of

the year. We had lost six of seven, and we had 31 games left. I think if I remember right, we needed 35 points to get to 97, which is what you estimate you need to get in.

We had the dads with us, and we were able to win in Nashville and the next one too, in Minny. We got our back end healthy coming out of the break, and that really helped solidify us. And we got Will Carrier back from an injury too.

JOHN STEVENS I'll never forget that game in Nashville. We won every puck battle. We were first on every puck – we just came out and played the game the right way. We won, and it wasn't even close. And we went right into Minnesota a day later and played the same way.

WILLIAM KARLSSON Dads' trips are fun because we're all together and it's like we're kids again with our parents at a tournament. The dads have so much fun. And a big part of the fun for us players is watching them enjoy themselves.

They put so much into our lives – hockey and otherwise – so you don't want to let them down. A lot of work goes into those trips. You want to reward them.

They've been pretty good luck for us over the years in Vegas. And we needed them this year. We weren't playing our best before that trip. But we were in a great mood, and the games were fun. We got our mojo back on that trip.

JACK EICHEL It's always a great time having the old men on the road. It's always funny to hear who the most hungover is in the morning and who made a fool of himself at the bar. I know my dad really enjoys it every season, and it seemed like they had a great group that really had fun together.

When you're enjoying time with your dad and with your teammates, it brings the group tighter. It was pretty cool to do that right after the bye week. We won two games, and it seemed like it sparked

VGK ORIGINS: JONATHAN MARCHESSAULT

Every player has a story. Every story has a beginning.

On February 24, the Vegas Golden Knights rolled out a 23-minute documentary about Jonathan Marchessault's journey from Cap-Rouge, Quebec, to Las Vegas. The piece was produced in-house by members of the Golden Knights storytelling team. Patrick Ruhlig and Jeff Chaves, who flew from Las Vegas to Quebec during the summer to spend time with Marchessault and his family, got to work telling the story of how an undersized forward worked his way to the NHL and eventually became a fan favorite with the Golden Knights.

"It didn't take long for Vegas fans to cling to Marchy for his talent on the ice and personality off the ice," Ruhlig said. "The opportunity to give fans a deeper look into his past and tell his story is one Jeff and I will cherish forever."

Hockey Hall of Famer Patrick Roy's presence in the documentary provided a unique perspective on Marchessault's upbringing in hockey. Roy, who won four Stanley Cups as a goaltender during his career, turned to coaching at the end of his playing days and coached Marchessault when he was with the Quebec Ramparts. He shared stories of drafting Marchessault in the

Quebec Major Junior Hockey League, and the forward's growth as a player and a person he witnessed.

"He was a leader on our team," Roy said. "Leaders, when they're positive and they're doing the right thing, you want them to lead. When you see them slipping, it's your job to make sure they're back on track."

As Marchessault started his professional career, he began two more full-time, lifelong jobs: husband and father. He met his wife, Alexandra, while he was playing in Hartford in the New York Rangers farm system. They fell in love and began their journey as parents when Marchessault was 23 years old. Family is the most important aspect of their lives as they raise their four children to uphold the same values.

"As a dad, he's very involved," Alexandra said. "He's really hands-on. He helps a lot, he's really funny, and he loves to play with the kids. I think he's a natural."

Marchessault's path through the AHL crossed with that of Ryan Craig, a player with the Springfield Falcons who went on to become an assistant coach with the Golden Knights. Craig stuck up for Marchessault on the ice when they were teammates, and their on-ice relationship

created a place of trust between them when Craig became his coach.

"The cool thing to watch after playing with him 10 years ago and coaching him for five years is his evolution," Craig said. "You mature with situations you go through in life. He's really earned everything he's gotten."

After parts of three seasons with the Tampa Bay Lightning and the Florida Panthers, Marchessault was selected by the Golden Knights in the 2017 Expansion Draft. The shock of moving his family to another city wore off quickly after he arrived in Vegas and became part of a special team destined for greatness. With a Stanley Cup and a Conn Smythe Trophy now on his résumé, the grinding toward greatness paid off for Marchessault and his family.

OPPOSITE
Former rival Jonathan Quick went 5-2-2 down the stretch for Vegas after his acquisition at the trade deadline.

our run to the end. We really enjoyed our time, and we know the dads did.

CRAIG We knew what was at stake when we returned, and I thought our focus was great. We were refreshed. We were ready to push, and, to tell you the truth, probably ready to play into June.

MCCRIMMON We went 22–4–5 the rest of the way. We held off Edmonton and LA in our division, but I think it was kind of underappreciated just how good the Western Conference was. Dallas, Minnesota, Colorado were doing the exact same thing.

Now, you're playing hard every game trying to win the division, but you're also hoping you can win the

conference. It seemed like games coming out of the break were pressure packed every single night. Every game was a big game right up until and including Game 82.

STONE Well, if you look at it, they're two different seasons. The first year I watched, we were losing. Those were the hardest two months of my life, probably, because you just want to do anything you can to help these guys. In the second year, it was hard to not be playing, and I'm sure the guys would have loved to have me out there. But they didn't really need me, the way we were playing. So that made it easier.

When you're sitting there watching, rehabbing – you're doing everything you can because you see

DEPTH CHARGE

Teams that have success have to lean on a long list of players to make it through an 82-game season.

The Vegas Golden Knights stayed healthier in 2022-23 than they had the year before, but the team needed to lean on its depth during the regular season to squeeze every point it could out of a grueling schedule. Vegas won the Pacific Division by two points, so each win collected along the way had great significance in the greater picture.

On Opening Knight against the Chicago Blackhawks, Vegas fed off the home crowd but had a tough time breaking through. Late in the second period, Paul Cotter wired his first goal of the season into the top corner to give the Golden Knights a 1-0 lead. Logan Thompson's 27-save shutout preserved the one-goal edge as Vegas picked up its second win in as many games to start the season.

Defenseman Daniil Miromanov played in 14 games for the Golden Knights in the 2022-23 season. As he filled in for injured teammates, Miromanov put together a three-point night on December 13 against the Winnipeg Jets that helped Vegas snatch a 6-5 victory. Two minutes after the Jets

opened the scoring, Miromanov potted his first NHL goal to get the visitors on the board. With the Golden Knights trailing, 4-3, in the third period, Miromanov set up Jonathan Marchessault twice for power play goals as the young defenseman helped spark the offense to a big win north of the border.

Another up-and-coming defender made contributions along the way, as Kaedan Korczak saw action in 10 games during the campaign. His first NHL point came on an assist to Nicolas Roy on January 2 in Colorado that helped the Golden Knights defeat the Avalanche, 3-2.

On March 12, 22-year-old Pavel Dorofeyev scored his first NHL goal in the third period against the St. Louis Blues to help Vegas secure a 5-3 win against the Blues. The game was the first NHL start for Jiri Patera, as the 24-year-old goaltender helped the Golden Knights pick up two points with just a month left in the regular season.

Dorofeyev shined on April 3 in Minnesota as his two-goal performance against the Wild drove the Golden Knights to a 4-3 shootout victory. His first goal came in the

second period to tie the game at 2-2. After the Wild took a 3-2 lead, Dorofeyev scored again in the final minute of regulation to force overtime. For an unofficial hat trick, Dorofeyev tacked on a goal in the fourth round of the shootout as Vegas turned what could have been a disappointing night into a two-point gain in the standings.

---

the team has a chance to win the Stanley Cup. And you feel like you could help out, so that makes you excited. Fortunately, we kept playing well, and that made rehabbing that much easier.

ADIN HILL We used five goalies. That's a lot. But every guy had success. LT was great early on. I had a strong start. Then when we got hurt – LB came on and was really the guy for a big part of the season. Jiri got a big win for us, and, of course, we added Quickie at the deadline.

We got four wins in a row from four different goalies. Turns out it's an NHL record. Never happened before. I didn't think about it at the time.

Bruce's system was good for us. And Sean Burke, I've known him a long time – he really kept us even keeled and focused. Quickie came in and

helped bring us even more together as a group. An incredible guy with a Hall of Fame résumé. It was great to just talk goalkeeping with him – even better to just hang out with him.

CASSIDY We didn't talk about first place all year. We talked about building our game so you're really good in April and May when you need it. Now, we are into April, and we said, "Let's win what's in front of us."

When we weren't practicing well, we'd go to compete drills. Our guys like to win. They're not as invested in some drills. But if we go to small ice games, they're locked in. Same with our schedule – whatever is in front of us, let's just win it. Our last 10 games, we had the chance to win the division and the conference. Our ability to win began to shine through.

OPPOSITE
Teddy Blueger proved to be a valuable addition after joining the team at the trade deadline.

DO IT FOR ANNABELLE

Spirits aren't as high when a team has lost three games in a row. It didn't happen often for the Vegas Golden Knights in 2022-23, but when the team dropped three straight in January, a pick-me-up was needed.

Enter Annabelle Hanson.

Through a partnership with Make-A-Wish Southern Nevada, Annabelle's dream of spending time with the Golden Knights and meeting her hero, Mark Stone, came true.

On January 20, Annabelle arrived at City National Arena for practice. She signed a one-day contract with the Golden Knights, shook hands with GM Kelly McCrimmon, and got to work with her new teammates with "Knight for Life" status.

Annabelle's mind went away from her struggles with cystic fibrosis and instead turned to gearing up for practice with her favorite team. She watched from the bench as the Golden Knights got to work preparing for a matchup against the Washington Capitals the following night. When the work was done, cheers emerged from the crowd and players alike as Annabelle took her first strides on the ice.

Her new teammates helped her take shots on Logan Thompson and rooted her on in a playful fight with Keegan Kolesar.

"She's awesome," Kolesar said. "The moment I met her, she had a big smile on her face and she was so happy to be here."

Annabelle stuck around the next day to watch the Golden Knights take on the Washington Capitals at T-Mobile Arena. When the starting lineups were announced, the crowd at The Fortress erupted when Annabelle stood alongside Thompson and was introduced to the fans. The Golden Knights routed the Capitals, 6-2, and gave credit for the win to their new teammate.

"I think everyone needed that," Thompson said. "The guys needed to have some fun, and putting a smile on her face is amazing. The guys love doing it, and we loved having her out. It's a big reason why you play the game – for moments like this."

Vegas – which had started the season 13-13-0 at home – was the best home team in the NHL from Annabelle's visit on. She attended two more playoff victories as well, including the Game 5 clincher against Florida.

OPPOSITE
Annabelle Hanson witnessed only wins in her visits to T-Mobile Arena during 2022-23.

We weren't perfect. No one called us a wagon during the regular season. They didn't call us a wagon until we steamrolled teams in the playoffs. We showed the ability to win and be good when we needed to. The coaching staff had to trust the players. They came through in crunch time.

ALEX PIETRANGELO If you look at our team and our season, no one jumps off the page. No 100-point guys. Instead, we won a lot of games.

Think of all the different people: Fourth line kicks in. Stevie is an All-Star. Marchy, Jack, and Barbie find something and dominate down the stretch. Karly

and Smitty play with different young guys. Stoney is hurt for a good stretch. Brett Howden and Michael Amadio become NHL regulars. Phil and Paul Cotter contributed.

I'll take our blueline over any in the NHL, but no one got any Norris Trophy buzz. Actually, none of our guys were up for any regular-season awards. We used five goalies. Our PP and PK numbers weren't great.

But we finished first in the West and played winning hockey from the All-Star break on. We figured out how to win as a team. And that made us unstoppable in the end.

SHOTS, SHOTS, SHOTS!!

BY LIL JON

It's unbelievable to me that Bill Foley said they would win the Stanley Cup in six years – and then it actually happened!

Supporting the Vegas Golden Knights is so important to me since this city is like my second home. I remember my first time coming to T-Mobile Arena to record promotional videos for the fans, and they only had one jersey made at the time!

I can remember the first season vividly. The Golden Knights had the best game-opening show in the league – the atmosphere was unmatched – and, honestly, those Knights games at The Fortress truly revitalized my love for hockey.

Fast-forward six years, and Vegas is back in the Stanley Cup Final! Throughout the entire Final, the team looked unstoppable!

Vegas came out, represented, and now the Golden Knights are NHL champions in 2023. Y'all brought that Stanley Cup home, and you earned it. I'm proud of the team for puttin' their everything into this season!

The boys took a lot of shots, shots, shots to get there, and I'm glad my coaching paid off – ha-ha-ha! I had a blast doing that skit, and we went *virallll!!!*

A new season is around the corner – *Let'ssss Goooooooooooo!!! YEAHHHHH!!!*

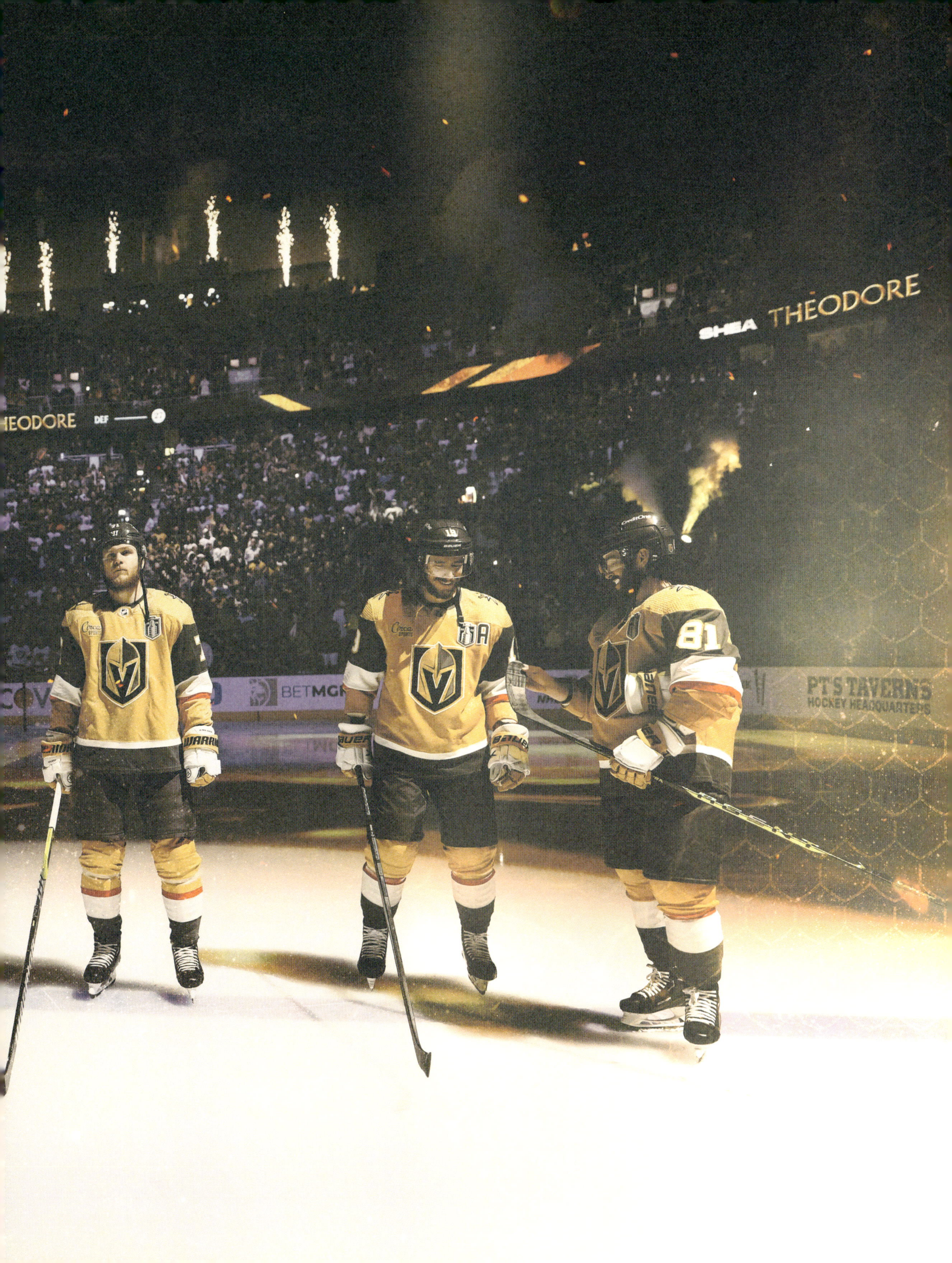
SHEA THEODORE
PT'S TAVERNS
HOCKEY HEADQUARTERS

THE
PLAYOFFS

The gauntlet of the Stanley Cup Playoffs is the biggest challenge
in hockey, if not all of sports. And time and again,
these Vegas Golden Knights rose to the challenge.

Four best-of-seven playoff rounds. Sixteen wins. One team wins the last game of the season and gets to skate with hockey's coveted 35-pound prize.

An impressive 16–6 mark with victories over the Jets, the Oilers, the Stars, and the Panthers made Vegas "not only a hockey town, but a championship town," in the words of NHL commissioner Gary Bettman, after a 9–3 stomping of the Panthers in Game 5.

The organization had built a strong playoff résumé, but ultimate success proved elusive through its first five years. Hockey Operations leaders George McPhee and Kelly McCrimmon had leaned into winning a championship, though, building a roster that would not be denied.

"Having such a good team and knowing that you have so many guys that could step up any night, it takes a lot of pressure off you personally and it allows you to just relax and play," said Jack Eichel after his first VGK playoff run. "We were deep, and we didn't care about individual stuff. We wanted to win, and nothing else mattered.

"We were driven, but we had leaders that made sure we were having fun. We didn't get crazy about losses. By the time we got back to the hotel after games, we were on to the next task. Between our veterans and the coaches, we were almost always in the right mindset. And when we slipped a bit, we were honest with one another about it.

"At the end of the day, it was a blast – the best couple months of my life. It was everything I wanted it to be, and more."

+ + + + +

ROUND 1
Golden Knights defeat Jets 4–1

Game 1 **Jets 5** Golden Knights **1**
Game 2 **Golden Knights 5** Jets **2**
Game 3 **Golden Knights 5** Jets **4** (2OT)
Game 4 **Golden Knights 4** Jets **2**
Game 5 **Golden Knights 4** Jets **1**

KELLY MCCRIMMON I had quite a bit of regard for Winnipeg. They had been in first place in the Central for around 83 days. They had a really good

The theme of the 2023 Stanley Cup Playoffs for Vegas was to UKnight fans across the Realm of Gold and Ice.

Mark Stone (center) scored two third-period goals in Game 2 versus Winnipeg, the first of four straight Vegas wins against the Jets.

plays in that game that I don't normally make. Just mental fatigue, almost.

Coming into the next game, I told myself, "I'm not going to be nervous. We have a great team. Just be part of that team." And that's what I did.

Four periods into the series, it looked like it wasn't gonna go great for us.

BRAYDEN MCNABB I think it was a little bit of feeling out, a little bit of "Oh we're in first place. It's not going to be hard. It's going to be easy." Honestly, our first four periods were bad. Game 2, the first period was bad, too. We got a little kick in the ass in the first intermission, and then it was game on after that.

JACK EICHEL I wasn't myself in Game 1. Neither was Stoney. The whole team was a bit off. But we got it going in Game 2. I scored. Stoney had a pair. Stevie scored too. That line was awesome in the game. We felt a lot better going up to Winnipeg with the series tied 1–1 and our captain looking like he was back in form.

MCCRIMMON Game 3 was a swing game in the series. Had we blown the 4–1 lead and lost in overtime, it's a real a tough one to overcome. It gives them all the momentum heading into Game 4. So the Amadio goal (in the second overtime of Game 3) was so important for us. It was one of the biggest goals of the playoffs, in my opinion.

MICHAEL AMADIO Obviously, you never want to give up a lead. We were up 3–0, and I think even 4–1 to start the third. It was unfortunate that we gave up those goals, but I think we knew that someone had it in our room.

It was a pretty special feeling – something that I will probably never forget – but I think it was a huge team effort. LB made some big saves to keep us in the game as well. It was a good game played by everybody.

BRUCE CASSIDY We played our best game of the series in Game 5. They really didn't have much of a chance. You need to win the first round if you're

start to the season, then they had a tough stretch. They have a Vezina-caliber goaltender as well.

But when we lost Game 1, I sure felt our foundation was strong enough that we would respond in Game 2. We had played a lot of really good hockey all through February, March, April. It's not a great feeling ever, but you get ready for Game 2, and that's what we did.

MARK STONE I was very nervous going into Game 1. I hadn't played since January, and now I was stepping into playoff hockey. We hadn't had a ton of practices, and I was taking a ton of blows. I knew that I was going to be targeted – I knew I was going to take some cross checks. And I was nervous.

Once I got comfortable with the hitting, I felt better. Honestly, my timing was off – I made some horrible

WELCOME TO THE FORTRESS

5 . . . 4 . . . 3 . . . Live from Las Vegas . . . It's Knight Time!

The Vegas Golden Knights have been known for their stellar in-arena entertainment experience since the team joined the NHL in 2017. The production that goes into each home game has only advanced each season, and the return to the Stanley Cup Playoffs brought the organization back on the national stage to show off the best atmosphere in professional sports.

An opportunity to pursue the Stanley Cup is one to celebrate, and the Golden Knights front office wanted every fan across the realm of gold and ice to come together in support of Vegas' team. "UKnight The Realm" became the battle cry as supporters around the world joined together to push Vegas to victory – and those in the arena became part of the show with their mobile phone flashlights.

Conquer the Skies
When the Golden Knights drew the Winnipeg Jets in the opening round of the Stanley Cup Playoffs, the entertainment team got to work on a pregame show that set the tone for the postseason. When the teams clashed in 2018, the battle climaxed with the Golden Knight splitting a jet in half. For their second playoff battle, the skating villain clad in black rushed onto the ice, proclaiming Winnipeg's aerial dominance. He was met by the Golden Knight, who raised the crowd to a level of sound that could summon a medieval beast capable of grounding a jet. From beneath the ice, a projected dragon burst through the frozen ground to bathe the plane in flames.

Striking Oil
Vegas turned its attention to Edmonton as the Golden Knights and Oilers clashed in the second round. The VGK production team used its best-in-class projectors to cover the ice in trebuchets controlled by the villain representing Edmonton. As he launched digital fireballs around the ice, the Golden Knight once again called on his dragon to lay waste to the enemy's equipment and defend the Fortress.

Quest for the West
With the north conquered, Vegas was one step away from the Stanley Cup Final. The audience at T-Mobile Arena went on a trip through space as ice projections resembled the passing of hyperspace as seen in a *Star Wars* film. Drummers clad in LED armor descended from the rafters and beat their drums as they dangled above the ice. On the surface of a distant planet, the villain and the Golden Knight did battle once again. A roar from the crowd signaled for the projected dragon to return to the ice surface and dispose of Vegas' foe once again.

Final Conquest
One team stood in Vegas' way in pursuit of the Stanley Cup: The Florida Panthers rallied their way through the Eastern Conference to face the Golden Knights in the Stanley Cup Final. A dense swamp was projected on the ice, and five villains emerged to outnumber the Golden Knight. Drummers rappelled from the rafters again and played on as the Golden Knight expelled his enemies until one remained. They engaged in bladed battle at center ice, and the Golden Knight thrust the villain down before his trusty dragon. The only roar louder than the dragon's was that of the 19,058 strong in attendance as they cheered their approval and rocked the Fortress as the eventual Stanley Cup Champion Golden Knights took the ice.

going to win the Stanley Cup. That's obvious, right? But lots of great regular-season teams get beat out in the first round. It happens. The 16 teams that make the playoffs are good teams.

JONATHAN MARCHESSAULT People don't know, but all my teammates know – me and Bruce went at it in the first round of the playoffs. We were disagreeing, and we were going at it. We were arguing for at least three games out of the five during the series. We were yelling at each other and all that. I guess it spiced up the guys at certain times, and he said that part of the reason was to spice up the team and make sure we have emotion out there.

I told him after the first round, "Let's not go another round like this. Just leave me alone. I know how to play the game. I don't tell you how to coach, but I know how to play the game. I've been in the NHL for a long time, and I've been a pretty good player. I know what to do – just leave me alone."

He left me alone, and we didn't argue one time after that. We just kept going with our playoff run, except the casual "Hello," "Good morning," and stuff like that. We didn't say anything to each other. That turned out being pretty good for me, and I'm sure he thought it was pretty good for him too.

ROUND 2
Golden Knights defeat Oilers 4–2

Game 1 Golden Knights **6** Oilers **4**
Game 2 Oilers **5** Golden Knights **1**
Game 3 Golden Knights **5** Oilers **1**
Game 4 Oilers **4** Golden Knights **1**
Game 5 Golden Knights **4** Oilers **3**
Game 6 Golden Knights **5** Oilers **2**

MCCRIMMON That was a hard series. It was a hard series, and every time you lost a game, you wondered if you could ever win another one. They won Game 2, and you're going, "Oh, my God."

BRAYDEN MCNABB We won Game 1 at home. We played pretty good. Their power play had been awesome in their first-round series with LA. Game 2, it exploded on us. It's funny – we weren't playing poorly on the PK, but everything went in for them.

They scored four in the first, and two were on the PP. They scored three on the PP that game. We knew we were in a series, and we had to slow down their power play. At five-on-five, we were fine.

MARCHESSAULT Game 3, we won 5–1, and I had two early. It was the start of some really good things for our line. Any goal scorer in NHL knows that when you get hot, you get hot. I was pretty cold in the first round, but I got hotter than burnt toast after, so I made up for it.

That's how it is in a season, though – when you're hot, you try to surf the wave as long as you can. When you're cold, you're trying to get out of it. No one talks about the stretch I had during the season, when I had three goals in 24 games. That was pretty bad for me. After you get out of your slump, you start being hot again, and you're good. It's the way it goes sometimes.

MCNABB We get the series lead back, but we lose the goalie we had been riding. Fortunately, we were kind of used to that by then, and had a lot of faith in Adin.

ADIN HILL You hate to see your teammate go down, right? It's always tough to see when you're sitting on the bench. It's a little different than when you see a goalie partner struggling, and the score's 3–0. And then he gives up a fourth, and you think you might be going in.

THE NEW DADS

In the spring of 2023, four members of the Vegas Golden Knights welcomed new children into the world.

Mark and Hayley Stone's family grew on March 20 with the birth of daughter, Scarlett. Brett and Meike Howden had their son, Charlie, on April 13. During the first round of the Stanley Cup Playoffs, Laken McNabb became the first child of Brayden and Lelanie McNabb. The youngest of the group, Beckham Karlsson, was born to William and Emily Karlsson on May 12 during the second round of the playoffs.

The excitement that comes from being a first-time father carried over to the ice during the playoffs. A week after his son was born, Howden had a two-goal performance in Game 4 against Winnipeg. After the game, he told VGK broadcaster Dan D'Uva about his first week of fatherhood.

"It was the best day of my life," Howden said. "He's only a week old now. I'm learning a lot as I go. It's the best thing that's ever happened to us, and every day is a great day."

Beckham Karlsson was born at 1:35 a.m. on May 12. Seventeen hours later, Vegas took on Edmonton in Game 5 of the second round and Beckham's father assisted on the go-ahead goal for the Golden Knights in a 4-3 win to take a 3-2 lead in the series.

"I didn't sleep too much last night, but I got a long nap in the afternoon," said William Karlsson. "I felt pretty good coming to the

game today. The win is a cherry on top – that's a good way to describe it."

A father of two himself, head coach Bruce Cassidy understands what the first-time parents were going through in the midst of a run to the Stanley Cup. He said the relief of a healthy family helps a player go into a game with a clear mindset, whether it's a regular-season game or a pivotal contest in the playoffs.

"It was a special day for him," Cassidy said of Karlsson after the Game 5 win over the

Oilers. "I think you're running on adrenaline then. Your baby and your wife are healthy. That always worries everybody. You come out of that part, and you're a dad. I think whether you sleep one hour or 10 hours, you're ready to go. You're just excited. Your life is better. It translates in your mindset coming onto the ice. It's worked well for us. It's baby number four. We may be calling the guys again in July or August and telling them, 'Let's get to work, fellas.' That's something to consider: a summer project."

When the guy is playing well and gets hurt, you're just thrown into it. You don't really have time to think. You just have to put your gear on and get out there, which I feel like sometimes can be better. In that moment, you just face that first shot, try and settle into the game, control your breathing a bit, and just focus on the job at hand.

Our guys have played in front of a few different goalies this year, and no matter who it was, we had success. I think that helped.

I went in cold in Game 3, and it went well. We won. Game 4, we got beat pretty good. They jumped on

us right off the bat, and we never responded. It got ugly at the end. Petro slashed [Leon] Draisaitl, and then [Darnell] Nurse jumped Nic Hague.

ALEX PIETRANGELO Here's my thing: Some of the stuff that happened to me or Stoney in that series, it was garbage. I know who we're playing, and you're letting them get away with it.

Did I want to hurt him? No, look, he's one of the top three, maybe five players in the world. I have nothing but respect for him, and I tried to apologize. But for me, it was like, you're going to take liberties on our best player and you're going to go after Stoney –

and they knew exactly where they were going after him, if you watch every time he was getting hit. They knew what they were doing.

So for me, it was just to send a message and be like, "Look, you're going to go after him. OK, well, we'll go after your best player." That's just the way it is. Did I need to go to that extreme? No, probably not. But I wanted to show my teammates that I'll do whatever I have to do to stick up for someone. I don't care what it is.

JOHN STEVENS It was unbelievable, the physical liberties that were taken against Petro. It tells you right there how important he is to our hockey team. But he is a true warrior. Everything he took, he gave back. He never backed down – he never gave up an inch of ground out there. But it was unbelievable, the liberties that were taken against him: cross checks to the head, cross checks after the play.

Petro got a game suspension for basically standing up for himself and his team. All we did was suck it up and win when our best defenseman was out of the lineup – just another indication of what our team was

all about. It killed Petro, not being in the lineup that game – to sit back and watch – but he's the first guy down there high-fiving guys when the game's over.

MCNABB There's definitely a little bit of an old-school approach there with Petro. I'm sure he was probably sick of getting run, and he took matters into his own hands. I don't think anyone held that against him – we respect Petro as a player and as a person. Maybe if you ask him, he wouldn't do it again. But maybe he would – I don't know.

MARK STONE The way I look at it, there was really only one game in the playoffs that felt like elimination. It was Game 5; if you lose that game, you're going into Edmonton down 3–2, and that's a tall task. For us to be able to get that game, especially without Petro, Hutty came in and did an incredible job of adding stability.

To lose one of your top defenseman, I think that is the hardest way to play against two of the best players on Earth and the best power play of all time. But we knew that if we could stay disciplined, our five-on-five game was superior.

Alec Martinez and the Vegas defense held the Oilers to five goals in Games 5 and 6 combined.

STEVENS To be honest, nobody could stop their power play. But we slowed it down in Games 5 and 6, and that was the series. As we moved through the series, I thought our guys did a better and better job of taking away the options that they wanted. But they're just so good at finding a wrinkle, if you make a little mistake, bad line change, poor clear – they just capitalize on it all the time.

The biggest thing was probably that we didn't take a lot of penalties late in the series. Our team is extremely disciplined. And the reason for that is, we check really well with our feet. We don't reach from behind and put referees in situations where they feel like they have to call a penalty. Our guys were extremely disciplined where they played really hard between the whistles and didn't carry it outside the whistles. And I thought that was huge for us in the Edmonton series.

Draisaitl had one point in the last four games. The guys did a good job, because he was their primary option on a seam. They took that away.

MCCRIMMON I remember Game 5 – I think it was a faceoff with maybe four seconds left, and you still weren't sure you're going to win that game.

CRAIG We came in after Game 5, and we had given up three PP goals, and we said our PK was unreal. It won us the game. And, you know, to me that's playoff hockey, right? It doesn't matter how you get it done. We just tried to win that game – and moved on to the next one.

STONE We have a big group – you're not going to push us around. Yeah, maybe we don't have a bunch of guys that are going to fight on the daily, but Keegan Kolesar had some big fights for us. Nicolas Hague had some big fights for us. It just shows we're not backing down. You can do whatever you want. You're not going to bother us.

We headed up there for Game 6, and the Misfits and Hilly put the series away. They scored two early on him, then he shut the door. And all five of our goals came from Misfits – three for Marchy, and Smitty and Karly both scored too.

We had some key kills at key times. Obviously, when we got that five-minute major, and to only give up one, we gained a lot of momentum. And once we started playing five-on-five in that game, I think that was the difference.

PIETRANGELO I felt like, watching that game, the guys were going to do whatever they could to win. I had so much faith that we were going to win that game because I felt like it kind of gave us a boost a little bit. That wasn't the intention, but I felt like guys were, like, "Let's do it for Petro, and let's make sure we win this game." I was sweating watching that game. I was so nervous. It was tough to watch.

AIKEN'S ASSIST

Equipment managers in the NHL just know. Their eyes are trained to see when something isn't quite right with a player's equipment, and they usually have a solution before a player even brings it up.

During Game 2 of the Stanley Cup Final with the Vegas Golden Knights leading, 3-0, in the second period, a puck glanced off Mark Stone's stick. J.W. Aiken, the team's assistant equipment manager, immediately recognized that the contact the puck made could have broken Stone's stick despite the fact that he continued using it. Aiken pulled a new stick for Stone from the rack just in case.

Sure enough, Stone leaned on his stick, and it snapped in two while the Florida Panthers were trying to generate offense in

Vegas' zone. Stickless, Stone threw a hit on Brandon Montour and raced to the bench, where Aiken was already reaching the new lumber out over the ice. Aiken had pushed his way from one end of the bench to the other to anticipate where Stone would be looking for it.

As Chandler Stephenson raced the puck through the neutral zone, he slipped a pass to Stone, who seamlessly joined the play. Without overhandling or overthinking, Stone snapped the puck to Brett Howden, who streaked through the middle of the ice, dragged the puck around Sergei Bobrovsky, deposited the puck into the open cage, and celebrated the goal with his teammates.

On the bench, assistant coach Ryan Craig gave Aiken a pat on the back and head

equipment manager Chris Davidson-Adams ran over to give him a fist bump. The goal was a difference maker, as the Golden Knights claimed victory in Game 2. Every contribution counts.

MCCRIMMON When William Karlsson scored into the empty net in Game 6 might have been the first time I was comfortable in the entire series.

WESTERN CONFERENCE FINAL
Golden Knights defeat Stars 4-2

Game 1	Golden Knights **4**	Stars **3**	(OT)
Game 2	Golden Knights **3**	Stars **2**	(OT)
Game 3	Golden Knights **4**	Stars **0**	
Game 4	Stars **3**	Golden Knights **2**	(OT)
Game 5	Stars **4**	Golden Knights **2**	
Game 6	Golden Knights **6**	Stars **0**	

STONE I thought the first game, we played well. They tie it up late, but we just stuck to it, got the early overtime winner. Game 2, probably not our best. I thought they sat back in the third period and tried to not give anything up, and we had a hard time getting through, but it was kind of like a boring third period. They make one mistake, and Marchy scores a huge goal for us. I figured if we could jump on them early in overtime, maybe jump on a mistake, we could get one early, and, sure enough, Stevie scores another huge goal for us.

WILLIAM KARLSSON We were really good in Game 3. Eichel's line had five points and three goals.

Two for Barbie. That got us up 3-0 in the series, but we lost our way for a bit after that and lost the next two. But Game 6, we were not to be denied.

STONE We had a great meeting the night before Game 6, about where we want to go, who we want to be. We were ready to go. We started our fourth line because of the energy that they bring to the team. That's Vegas Golden Knights hockey, right? To get those four lines going, get to see six D chipping in and get Adin with a shutout. That was probably a poster game – I think our coaching staff will probably show us clips from that one next year.

CASSIDY We had a meeting the night before, which I don't typically do. I put some clips together to show the guys about an hour before the meeting. They weren't pretty. We were losing the slot battle and getting pushed around in front of our net. I said that if we don't address this, we can't just let it slide here, because it's 3-2 now in the series.

My tone was probably – I don't want to say negative, but going at them. I knew we were going to challenge the players, and then we're going to have another conversation and appeal to them.

Do you want to be a Stanley Cup champion, or not? You've been this far before. Some have won, and some haven't. "Hey, Chandler, you got over the hump in Washington, and it took you guys a long time, right? Remember what that felt like?" So I'm asking these rhetorical questions and talking about the three or four winners in the room.

Then you're pointing out the five or six that lost in a Final – and I put myself in that group. I'm with you guys – I'm with the Misfits. I was that close too, and I don't want to mess it up again. There was probably a little bit of emotion in my voice because it still bothers me that we lost. You're appealing to the guys, you're pushing the guys, but you're also in there with them.

We basically touched the whole group with that meeting, and it was probably 15 to 20 minutes. The reason I know it was successful is guys were all paying attention and nodding their heads. You could tell the guys were thinking through the message and how it affected them. Every guy in that room was thinking about it a little bit differently.

We left there with a common goal that we're going to get it done tomorrow. We need to get back to our game and play our best game of the playoffs, and we did.

CRAIG The coaches met before and went over the clips of what Bruce was going to show. And then we briefly talked about what his topic was going to be. *Legacy* was probably the word that stood out for players. But those aren't rehearsed. You maybe have an idea of which way it's going to go down. We knew what was going to be spoken of. You just didn't know the emotional part of it that can come out when you have a meeting like that.

STEVENS That game was never going to be in question. But I thought the way he delivered that message was able to kind of temper his emotions because we're all getting to the point where we want to get to the Final. That, to me, might have been his best coaching of the entire playoffs in that meeting.

HILL That game has to be the easiest shutout of my career – in the NHL, definitely. I think they might

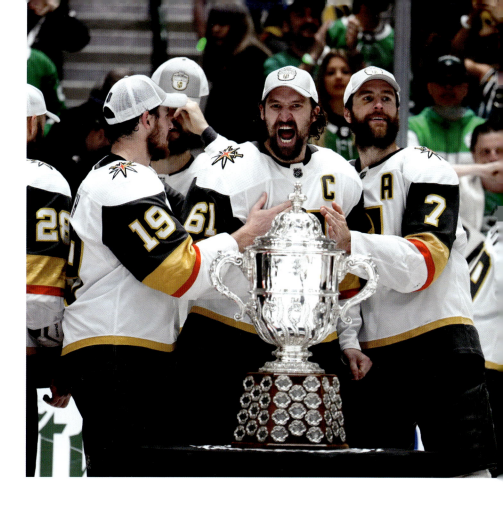

have had two or three grade-A chances all game. I'm guessing; I don't know the real stat. But they weren't a breakaway or anything like that. They were more like power play plays.

I thought that game was truly remarkable, the way our team stepped up and all four lines are going. We didn't let them breathe.

Mark Stone roared behind the Clarence S. Campbell Bowl after a dominant 6–0 Golden Knights win in Game 6 at Dallas.

STANLEY CUP FINAL
Golden Knights defeat Panthers 4–1
Game 1 Golden Knights **5** Panthers **2**
Game 2 Golden Knights **7** Panthers **2**
Game 3 Panthers **3** Golden Knights **2** (OT)
Game 4 Golden Knights **3** Panthers **2**
Game 5 Golden Knights **9** Panthers **3**

EICHEL I didn't really know what to expect, because they had just beat three really good teams. I knew how good we were, but I just thought this could be a really tough series for us. Ultimately, it ended up not being that tough. We had a great hockey team, and we were better than them. I don't care if they are healthy or banged up. We were a better hockey team.

I remember Shea Theodore texted me when Boston lost, and he said, "This is our year." It was either after

PREGAME ON THE PLAZA

Vegas Golden Knights fans latched on to the excitement of the team's run in the Stanley Cup Playoffs. Hours before they entered T-Mobile Arena for each game, they gathered on Toshiba Plaza outside the arena, where the organization created an atmosphere that got the party started well before puck drop.

With music bumping, face painting, free haircuts, and food and beverages being enjoyed outside the arena, fans arrived eager to be part of the fun before the emotional roller coaster the postseason brings. Inkmaster Joey Hamilton and his team from Revolt Tattoos set up outside of every home game to provide complimentary Golden Knights tattoos for fans looking to add to their collection of body art. The primary VGK shield, the intersecting swords of the secondary logo, and the Reverse Retro-style diagonal *Vegas* were among the permanent signals of team loyalty that Golden Knights fans had tattooed on their bodies.

Marshmello got the festivities underway in the Stanley Cup Final as the popular DJ performed a set on Toshiba Plaza prior to Game 1. Above the arena, skywriters displayed the city's passion for its team by adding some VGK-themed cloud coverage for fans before they went inside for the game. Ahead of Game 5, Steve Aoki performed for the crowd and made sure every fan was

properly hyped up before a military flyover that prompted the arena doors to open.

"What has happened here has been simply incredible," NHL Commissioner Gary Bettman said while presenting the Stanley Cup. "Not only is Vegas a hockey town, it's a championship town."

When the games got underway, fans without tickets remained outside the arena, where each contest was shown on the screen above the Allegiant Stage. Crowds on Toshiba Plaza swelled as the postseason continued on and fans united to watch the Golden Knights on their quest for the Stanley Cup regardless of the temperature outside.

As the 19,058 fans inside the arena celebrated at the end of the clinching game in the Stanley Cup Final, the crowd of up to 20,000 supporters outside the arena roared their approval as the Golden Knights made history. The Stanley Cup celebrations took over the city, and the party that began ahead of Game 1 of the first round reached its peak when the greatest trophy in sports was handed to Mark Stone.

"Vegas, you certainly know how to throw a party," Bettman said on the ice. "What's going on inside this arena and outside is incredible and a testament to what a great hockey market this is."

---

the Boston loss or when we beat Edmonton, and he texted me out of the blue and said, "This is our year." When you get a group of guys that have belief in themselves, that just goes so far, and it did for our group.

When we went to the Final, scoring five and seven goals on them in Game 1 and Game 2, after that, we knew we were so much better than them.

STONE Hiller's save in Game 1 on [Nick] Cousins, that could have changed the series. You don't know exactly what could happen after, because it didn't happen, right? If they go up 2–1 there, they're starting to feel pretty good about themselves, they

got the lead, but he makes that save, and it's a wild moment – deflates their bench and juices up ours.

I think then Theo scores that incredible goal shortly thereafter and just brings so much energy. Those kinds of saves at those kinds of times, maybe as crazy as it sounds, it can change the series.

ALEC MARTINEZ With Adin Hill, it was a defining moment seeing him just stepping in and being as good as he was. That's entirely another book, but the one that sticks out in my mind is Game 1 against Florida. The Save. The picture that's everywhere of him sprawling out, that was a series-defining moment.

OPPOSITE
Chandler Stephenson (left) and Shea Theodore celebrated Stephenson's Game 2 overtime goal versus Dallas.

ABOVE
When Adin Hill made the Save in Game 1, Florida and Vegas were tied, 1-1, early in the second period.

OPPOSITE
Brett Howden scored two goals in the 7-2 Game 2 victory, earning the postgame Elvis wig and sunglasses in the locker room.

It's hard to find the balance. You don't want to micromanage or get worked up about any particular play or mistake, or anything like that. But oftentimes, it is those little plays. I think that without Hill's save in the Cup Final, that could have been a very different series.

MCCRIMMON Adin Hill was exceptional, and a lot has been made about our system and it being goalie friendly, and those types of things. I think that sells Adin short. I think Adin made some incredible saves at very important moments to help our team win. He made so many great saves. He was big and in position and competitive. He stopped the puck. He was very, very good.

MARCHESSAULT We were too much for them. We beat them, 5-2 and 7-2, in the first two games. They were trying all that crap after the whistle, and we were just scoring goals. They had the big hit on Eichel, and they yapped about it. Kolesar destroyed [Matthew] Tkachuk in Game 3, and we didn't say a word. Yeah, we lost Game 3. But it just set us up to be able to win the Cup at home.

EICHEL I thought we played a great Game 3. They threw everything at us – they get a big goal late and obviously went into overtime. It's a little bit deflating because we felt like we played a good game, and we were two minutes away from going up, 3–0.

I thought the message to the group was the same: "Hey, we played a great game. The bounces didn't go our way. Let's regroup and just put our best foot forward here for Game 4. We've been the better team in the series. We're the deeper group – we're very confident in where we're at and just got to go win Game 4." Which we did.

MCCRIMMON Flying home from Florida, up 3–1, I expected us to win the Stanley Cup.

CASSIDY Just a gut instinct. Figured I'd start the Misfits – I had a good feeling about the game. I think our guys were ready to win. You're going into Game 5, and you have a chance to win the Stanley Cup. So as a coach, someone will probably ask you that in an interview. What are you going to say to the guys in the most important game of the year?

Alec Martinez's Game 5 goal made the score 3–1 for Vegas on the way to a 9–3 victory.

You're looking for your 16th win? What are you going to say? And I'd be, like, "Jeez, I don't know."

Everyone knows the importance of that game, so what do you come up with? And I thought, *You know what? I'm not going to say anything. I'm just going to start those guys and talk about them being the foundation. They're the beginning, and tonight is the end. OK, you guys get to finish what you started.*

So that was kind of the speech I was looking for, but I knew I'd get emotional doing it, so I dummied that down. We would not talk about nerves or expectations. We're going to talk about the original guys and what they did for this franchise, and we're going to give them the first crack at it tonight, and off we go.

I didn't think we started the game that great, but I'm glad I put them out there. It wasn't their fault. I think they'll remember it for a long time, and they should. They earned it, deserved it.

BILL FOLEY Wasn't that something else? It was fantastic. I thought Butch made a genius move when he did that – five of the six guys from year one to start the game. Marchy, Reilly, and Karly. Nabber and Shea. And he recognized Will Carrier in the dressing room. Everyone recognized it.

The people who've been in the stands long enough all recognized it, and that was terrific. It was the acknowledgment to the 2017–18 team that came out of nowhere to almost win the Stanley Cup, and he puts the original five guys back out on the ice.

It was great. I thought that was a genius move; never would I have thought to do it. But that's Butch. He's a catch. He's the coach. A smart guy.

STEVENS We knew Florida would come out and play loose. They had nothing to lose, but neither did we. We were up in the series, and we deserved to be. And if you remember that first five to eight minutes of that game, they came at us hard. They had some great scoring chances, Hilly made some big saves, and then we just caught our stride. And we just knew that the outcome was never going to be questioned.

CRAIG Guys were OK talking about what was at stake. The task that was in front of us, there was no hiding from it, I guess. We knew that we deserved to be there. We knew that we deserved to have a chance to end the series in Game 5 at home.

MARTINEZ We needed to settle down, and who else but our captain? Stoney scored the shorty, and we were on our way. We were dominant. They couldn't get the puck out of their zone.

EICHEL A hat trick in the Stanley Cup clincher. Who does that? Mark Stone. He's our leader, and he took that game into his own hands. He wasn't going to be denied. He was fantastic.

I've never seen an environment like that. I've never seen a second period quite like that, or a stretch of hockey like that in general. I can't imagine what that felt like after all the crap that he's been through the last year and a half with back surgeries. To be able to do that and put the series and Stanley Cup in our hands must have been so great. As his teammate, you can't be happier for a person like that. He deserved it.

Such a cool moment, having a clinching hat trick and for our group to score nine goals. In the third period, I wished they would just run the time.

PLAYOFF WATCH PARTIES

The Vegas Golden Knights made sure fans had somewhere to gather when the team was on the road during the Stanley Cup Playoffs. Vegas fans flocked to the team's official watch parties around town to be together for the emotional highs and lows. Each party created a scene of support that was so uniquely Vegas.

The doors to The Dollar Loan Center in Henderson were opened for fans to watch the first road game of the Stanley Cup Playoffs at the home of the Henderson Silver Knights. Cheers erupted from the new 5,500-seat arena when Michael Amadio scored in double overtime to secure a Game 3 win for Vegas in Winnipeg. Two days later, fans took in the Game 4 action at Stadium Swim at Circa Resort & Casino to watch the game on the 40-foot-tall screen.

As the Golden Knights took on the Edmonton Oilers in the second round, the fun resumed as fans got back in the pool at Stadium Swim to watch Vegas' 5-1 win in Game 3. The swimsuits got more use for Game 4 as the team hosted a watch party at the Sandbar at Red Rock Casino, Resort & Spa. The lounge chairs were packed with fans decked out in gold in support of the Golden Knights. The final watch party of the second round returned to the Dollar Loan Center as Vegas vanquished Edmonton to reach the Western Conference Final.

As the playoffs continued, watch party attendance continued to swell. The city was behind its team, and it showed when the Golden Knights were on the road; for Game 3 of the Western Conference Final, massive screens were set up on the Lawn at Downtown Summerlin for fans to unite and watch the Golden Knights take a 3-0 lead in the series in a beautiful outdoor setting. Fans headed back down to the Strip for Game 4 as Mandalay Bay Beach became packed with fans of all ages decked in gold. The party returned to Stadium Swim for Game 6 as a 6-0 win for the Golden Knights propelled them to the Stanley Cup Final.

Vegas played two road games in the final series, but the parties were aplenty. As the Golden Knights took the ice in Florida, fans cheered from Stadium Swim and Downtown Summerlin. In the final road game of the run, Golden Knights fans packed the Las Vegas Ballpark to watch from the stands and from on the field. On the other side of town, Water Street Plaza in Henderson turned gold with supporters as Vegas defeated Florida, 3-2, to head home with a 3-1 lead and the Stanley Cup in their sights.

We were sitting there, and I was biting my jersey between periods. How am I going to play this 20 minutes here? We just need to get to the end of it. The hat celebration with all the hats on the ice, it was such a cool moment. It was like a pause before we celebrated, where we had our celebration between ourselves on the bench. It was, like, holy, we have to wait a couple more minutes here, but we just did it. We just won the Stanley Cup.

STONE When we were sitting in the locker room and the score was 6–1, 99 percent of me thought, "We've won the Stanley Cup." But then there was 1 percent of me that thought, "If we lose this game, that's gonna be one of the biggest debacles." I think once we scored the eighth goal, and then there was a TV timeout, we were all just kind of sitting on the bench with five minutes left. And you could kind of see both teams skating and winding out the clock. Sitting on the bench and looking around. Yeah, I'd say that last TV timeout, when the game kind of slowed down, that's when I knew that we were winning.

GEORGE MCPHEE You know, when you've been in the business for 40 years, and when this is your

THE MEAL ROOM

Each team in the NHL has a dedicated meal room on the road where they can get together at the hotel to eat together. In the playoffs, to only call it "the meal room" would be to call T-Mobile Arena "the hockey room."

The rooms are hotel ballrooms equipped with seating for the team's travel party and a spread of food that will help the players perform. You'll find chicken and vegetables before burgers and fries, as the team sticks to a diet that promotes energy and efficiency. But in the spring, eating is only a part of what goes on in that team space; as the players chase the Stanley Cup, the meal room becomes more of a multipurpose room and a space for team chemistry to blossom.

At breakfast time, forward Paul Cotter called it a quiet scene as the group gets the day started with a healthy meal and a cup of coffee. But when the team gets back after practice to eat lunch together, the real fun begins.

"When we get back, it's pretty much straight to the meal room, where guys will play poker, some guys will play little putt-putt games with each other," Cotter said. "There's a different game at each different hotel. It's pretty awesome."

The equipment staff travels with a putter, a tiny tin cup, and golf balls to transform the meal room into a makeshift Augusta National for a few hours. Chairs are positioned strategically to set up difficult shots as players challenge each other to reach the hole in as few strokes as possible.

If the ball kicks under the table where a poker game is being held, it must be played as it lies. Tricky shots through Brayden McNabb's feet or around Jonathan Marchessault's backpack have to be taken into account as the playful game is played under a serious set of rules.

After road games in the playoffs, the Golden Knights returned to the hotel, changed from their suits into sweatshirts and shorts and gathered for their postgame meals. When the team lost a game, the opportunity to get together as a group softened the blow and allowed them to refocus for the next one. After wins, the good vibes carried from the locker room to the meal room.

"The significance of winning in playoffs and being able to all take a breath together was huge," Cotter said. "To get together and play cards, knowing that we just got a big win, is a pretty awesome feeling."

The confines of the meal room have even been used for chaotic soccer games and accuracy challenges with a dartboard and a plastic axe. Whether you had a hat trick in that night's game or you were a healthy scratch, everyone has the same competitive spirit in a game of mini golf or Connect 4.

"I think that's Jonathan Quick's favorite part about this job," Cotter said. "He's the guy that's the last to leave because he's been telling stories and shooting the breeze with everybody. Those are some of the best times."

fourth time to the Stanley Cup and you haven't won, and you've experienced some heartbreaking losses and eliminations with teams that you thought were real good – that feeling of having a lead can evaporate.

And we were up 6-1. So you think before the third period, "This is going to be OK." And then the other team scores a couple of goals, and it's not OK. When we scored that ninth goal, that's OK – we have enough of a lead to try and let it go. But I do think that, after 63 days of playoffs and trying to stay in the moment, it's hard to let it go because you're wound up pretty tight during that whole period. And lots of people can say this – it doesn't quite feel real.

EICHEL It didn't matter to us who won the Conn Smythe. If Adin Hill had won it, I don't think anyone would have questioned it. He was unbelievable. If Mark Stone had won it, it would have been,

"He deserved that – he just had a hat trick, and he was phenomenal the entire playoffs."

It was really cool to see Jonathan win it, for a number of reasons. One, I just think of what he means to the team. Obviously, having been here from day one – and we always want to talk about the Misfits – you can give those guys so much credit for what they've built in terms of culture, the way that things are run around here. But I just think in general, what he means to the group, his personality every day, and the energy he brings.

MARCHESSAULT That's the thing about our team: It could have been anyone. And no one would have cared. I thanked Jack after they announced my name – told him, "I couldn't do this without you." But this trophy wasn't the one that mattered. Our team won the Stanley Cup. Our team. And when Stoney went up there to get it, that was the greatest moment for all of us. We won. VGK. Stanley Cup champs.

FEEDING THE BEAST

BY KERRY BUBOLZ

As anyone who has watched playoff hockey knows, the intensity level cranks up on the ice.

For those of us on the business side of the Vegas Golden Knights, we know we have to elevate the fan experience as well – we call it Feeding the Beast.

The Stanley Cup Playoffs are a Beast. They ask more of everyone in an organization, and I'm proud of how we delivered in 2023.

Take our game presentation, for example. It's already heralded as the best in the NHL, if not in all sports, so it's a challenge to that group when I tell them they've got to Feed the Beast and make it even better.

Their efforts started as soon as we clinched a spot in the playoffs, fittingly with a literal beast. As fans came to games, they saw a huge wooden box on Toshiba Plaza. If they looked closely and picked up on some clues, some deduced that there was probably a dragon inside.

We introduced the dragon to the pregame show for the first playoff game. We also added a new light show that engaged the crowd at The Fortress more than ever and perfectly fit our UKnight The Realm theme. As we progressed, we added drummers descending from the rafters, new on-ice graphics, and more celebrities to crank the siren than we had ever had before. What fans saw the night the team clinched the Cup on June 13 was on a whole other level from a regular-season show that already set the standard in the industry.

It showed elsewhere in the organization as well. Our graphics packages inside and outside the arena were beautiful. Battle Towel giveaways at every game contributed to the UKnight The Realm

storyline, with the support of our partners. We had tattoo artists, dunk tanks, and Steve Aoki on the Plaza. We had skywriters and military flyovers. We always want our games to be a spectacle that is fitting for our city, and I believe they have been.

Before you woke up every morning, our broadcasters published a new podcast – for 59 straight days. Our practices at City National Arena were electric, with appearances from our Cast and huge crowds. When the team was on the road, our watch parties took advantage of beautiful settings around the city and maintained

the local energy of our home games. New items were available at our stores every day. We had new streetlamp signs around T-Mobile Arena and VGK graphics on the marquees on the Strip.

The entire Valley was consumed by the quest for the Stanley Cup. We needed to elevate our game to match that, just like the team did on the ice – we had to Feed the Beast.

THE STANLEY CUP

It's every young player's dream to hoist the Stanley Cup. When they achieve that goal, whether they've been chasing it for 18 years or 80, the powerful emotions that are unleashed can be difficult to describe.

Vegas Born. It's the best way to describe what the Golden Knights mean to Las Vegans. This team is of this city and for this city. There is a bond between the people who live and work here. And the Stanley Cup is another link that connects the team with the town. The players earned this championship, but they didn't do it alone. Fans are the lifeblood of the Golden Knights.

Winning is no accident. It takes an owner willing to devote resources. Architects with a plan. Coaches and players elite in their fields. There must be synchronicity from top to bottom. And, goodness knows, there needs to be luck. Everything must fall into place to put a hockey team and its fanbase on top.

Bruce Cassidy told his players, "It hurts to win." They lived his credo. They absorbed the pain. They made the sacrifices. And they won. They became, as Mark Stone told his teammates late on the night of June 13, "the greatest hockey team in the world."

+ + + + + +

GEORGE MCPHEE Is it nice to have your name on the Stanley Cup? Yes. But it's not an everyday part of your life. It's nice to have a Stanley Cup ring; we all like to have one of those. But why is it important? I think, to me, it's what you can do for a community. And I love that we're able to do it for this community because of what this community had been through early in our history, and how much this team has been supported by this community.

I remember the civic pride that you could feel when you talk to people in Vegas. Whether you were in a taxi or a real estate agent was showing you around, people were happy that the city felt a little more legitimate now that they had their own pro team. People in Vegas love sports. They just had to love other teams – they didn't have their own. They had to look at other cities to find teams that they would support, and now they didn't have to do that anymore. And they supported this team so much. This team has been really good, but you need to win

Mark Stone, the only team captain in Golden Knights history, had nine points in the Stanley Cup Final, with at least a point in each game.

135

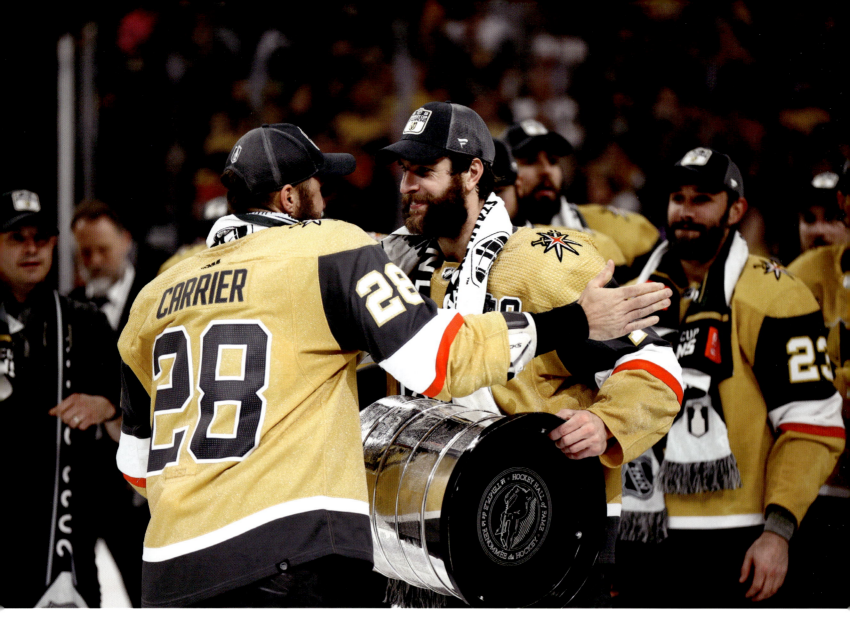

ABOVE
After all six Golden Misfits hoisted the Cup, William Carrier (left) passed it to alternate team captain Alex Pietrangelo.

OPPOSITE
Bruce Cassidy raised the Cup one day shy of a year after he was hired in Vegas.

it all to make it special. So we made it special for Las Vegas forever. For as long as we live. What we did was really unique and special for Las Vegas.

BILL FOLEY It's really the culmination of all of our goals from when we got the franchise. I didn't really think about that statement – "Playoffs in three, Cup in six." And then, of course, we're in the playoffs in one and were in the Stanley Cup Final in year one.

But I didn't make the statement to be arrogant or egotistical. I made the statement knowingly, which a lot of people didn't really think I did, I made it knowingly. Because I thought it might help the team to understand that there's a big goal here. And we expect to have things happen. And I expect all of you to participate in achieving our goal of winning the Stanley Cup.

I picked year six, because I thought that would give us enough time to bring enough new players in on top of the players we already had to create a team that could win. I didn't contemplate at the time that we would be in the conference finals four times in the first six years. That really was beyond my thought process.

BRAYDEN MCNABB Being an original guy, being here since day one, seeing the organization go through ups and downs – starting Game 5 meant a lot, and I'm sure those other four guys would say that. I wish Will Carrier could have been out there. I know Butch apologized to him – it would have been nice to stick him in the net if we could, but it was a cool moment for us.

Honestly, when I first got picked up, I just wanted to make the team – that was my goal. I actually didn't think I was going to, but obviously, it ended up working out pretty good. Just going through the whole building the organization, the October 1 shooting, doing all that stuff, and to ultimately win a

'MISFITS TO CHAMPIONS'

The clock began to wind down in Game 5 of the Stanley Cup Final. The game had been all but over for an hour already. Vegas led Florida, 9-3, in the final minute of the game, and on the other side of the boards at T-Mobile Arena, the Stanley Cup was being polished for presentation.

It was the 104th game of the season for the Vegas Golden Knights. It had taken them 22 games to complete the quest for the Stanley Cup after successfully navigating the 82-game regular season.

Game 5 was also the 104th broadcast of the year for Golden Knights radio play-by-play broadcaster Dan D'Uva. With help from Gary Lawless and Darren Eliot throughout the season, D'Uva's voice has carried Golden Knights hockey on the radio since the very first puck drop in 2017. As the dreams of the players were realized, D'Uva had the floor.

The Final Call
A minute to go in the third period of Game 5. Golden Knights 9, Panthers 3. The Knights are this close. We think about that first game in Golden Knights history. We think about that incredible ride that was the inaugural season. Bill Foley had asked the team to get to the playoffs in three years. They had done better than that. The noble charge from Bill Foley was "Cup in six." They talk about dreaming. The Golden Knights are going to make that dream a reality.

A devotion to destiny. Misfits to champions. The Golden Knights win the Stanley Cup in 2023!

The first Stanley Cup championship in Golden Knights history comes in their sixth season. The Silver State is home to the greatest silver trophy in all of sports.

The mob is behind Adin Hill's goal. All the players swarming one another jubilant in celebration. The fans, on their feet, can't stop. The streamers down from the rafters. Sticks and gloves and flamingoes. The Golden Knights are Stanley Cup Champions.

Every player managed to contribute. Each player played his part, and there the honor lies. Final score in Game 5: the Golden Knights 9, the Florida Panthers 3. They defeat Florida in five games to win the Stanley Cup, having knocked out the Stars in six, the Oilers in six, and the Jets in five. The Golden Knights win 16 out of 22 games in the Stanley Cup Playoffs to win the Stanley Cup in their sixth season on this Tuesday, the 13th day of June 2023.

Stanley Cup in year six when Bill said, "Cup in six" was pretty cool.

JONATHAN MARCHESSAULT I'm 32 years old, but I was like every kid playing in the street. I fulfilled my dream, and I'm lucky I did it at 32 years old. Some people's dream is own a house, own a boat, or something particular. My dream was to win a Stanley Cup, and I did it. I've won, and you can't take that away. It's hard to explain, but if I retire tomorrow, I've already fulfilled my dream. I've done what I wanted to do on this earth, professionally. Seriously, it's unbelievable. It's just hard to explain.

WILLIAM KARLSSON When I was a kid, I wanted to win the Stanley Cup, but I think an Olympic medal with Sweden would have ranked higher – but I don't know. Nowadays, the Stanley Cup means so much to me, and I'm super happy that we won. I think I would rank it the highest, even if I were to ever win a gold medal with Sweden in the Olympics.

KELLY MCCRIMMON In the moment, and in the short term, it's the exhilaration of winning a championship. The broader perspective, it was really

validation that so many of the decisions we had made over seven years were the right ones. We were resolute in our vision of what a championship team needed to look like, what type of players it needed to consist of, what type of identity was needed to be a champion, what type of character was needed to be a champion.

We stood by our beliefs and never wavered. We had an unwavering belief that we were making good decisions consistently. It's not just one – it's a series of good decisions over an extended period of time: That's how you get to this point of being a champion.

I've talked many times before about my happiness for all the other people who have worked, in many cases since Day 1, to get here. So that part is meaningful. On a personal level, it's incredibly gratifying that 34 years after my late brother Brad's name went on the Stanley Cup, mine is on the Stanley Cup.

In terms of, what did it mean? I've been in the game a long time. I rode the bus in the Western Hockey

The players waited arm in arm for the presentation of the Stanley Cup.

KOLESAR DOES IT FOR DAD

Families flooded onto the ice after the Vegas Golden Knights won the Stanley Cup. Mothers and fathers hugged their sons. Brothers and sisters celebrated with their champion siblings. Wives and girlfriends shed tears of joy with their husbands. Kids tried to understand what Dad had just accomplished.

Charles Peterson wasn't there. But his son, Keegan Kolesar, felt his father's presence on the ice when he realized his childhood dream of winning the Stanley Cup.

"I know he'd be jumping up and down for everyone here," Kolesar said. "I just look up

and know he's looking down. I'm so proud I could do this, and I know he'd be proud of me too."

Peterson passed away during the COVID-19 pandemic. While his father watches from above, Kolesar knows he's still very much a part of everything he's accomplished in his hockey career.

Kolesar was asked what he'd say to his dad if he could share a conversation with him after winning the Stanley Cup. His response: "Would you believe it? Would you [bleeping] believe it?"

League for 27 years. I was a day one employee in Vegas with George.

The other thing that that is unique, unless Seattle does the same, it's never happened that a management team made every single decision from inception to Stanley Cup champion. There have been some GMs that moved to different franchises – they step into the shoes of the person that was there before them. That wasn't the case for George and me – the fact that we were able to do that, to sort of be the architect of the entire process.

MARK STONE I was excited, for sure. I could not wait to get up there. My mind was racing, and I wasn't really hearing what Gary Bettman was saying. Once he called me up to receive the Cup, it was hard to look at the camera for that picture because all my teammates were standing there.

Just look at how excited everybody was to get that thing in the air and hoist the Stanley Cup over our heads. When I was able to pick up the Stanley Cup and look at my teammates, George, Kelly, all the coaching staff, Bill, all the medical guys, equipment guys, everybody standing there had a piece of it, and it was just awesome to be able to just pick it up and just look in the team's eyes and then go for a lap. And then, once the handoff, started that's

a special, special thing, being able to hand it off, because you hand it to the guy you're closest with. So it's pretty cool.

MCPHEE Personally, as Kelly likes to say, when we get too wrapped up in things, we have to remind ourselves, this is a game we played when we were five years old for fun. And it couldn't be more true. We grew up watching this game, knowing this game. We knew about the Stanley Cup when we were eight or nine years old. We knew what that was. And so, like a lot of kids, we grew up wanting to be an NHL player.

I got a chance to do that for a little while, and it was great. Naturally, what comes next is, you'd love to be able to win a Stanley Cup. And I heard it, but I like repeating it: I guess it's never too late to become what you always wanted to be, and I wanted to be a Stanley Cup champion. It took another 40 years, but I got to be a Stanley Cup champion.

And what it does, really, is, it almost erases anything negative in hockey in the past. When you lift the Stanley Cup up, you're in a pretty exclusive club. But it's all of the people that reach out to you as it's happening and after it happens – relatives, friends, people you haven't heard from in 30 or 40 years that somehow find you. What a great thing to experience in your life.

OPPOSITE
Original Golden Knight Reilly Smith (right) received the Cup from team captain Mark Stone.

STONE TO THE MISFITS

The first pass of the Stanley Cup from captain to worthy teammate creates an iconic moment every time the greatest trophy in sports is won.

Joe Sakic to Ray Bourque. Steve Yzerman to Vladimir Konstantinov. Scott Niedermayer to Rob Niedermayer.

Mark Stone to the Golden Misfits.

When Vegas' captain received the Stanley Cup from Gary Bettman, he took it for a skate through center ice at T-Mobile Arena. In the 30 seconds that Stone held the trophy, the question that passed through the minds of spectators was, "Who will he pass it to first?"

While Reilly Smith was the next individual recipient of the trophy, he was the first of a special group of six players who followed their captain in skating the Stanley Cup around the ice they once took in 2017 with heavy hearts and scattered expectations.

Smith, Jonathan Marchessault, William Karlsson, Brayden McNabb, Shea Theodore, and William Carrier were the six remaining players from the inaugural season of Golden Knights hockey in 2017-18.

"I didn't expect that, to be honest, because we have a lot of veterans on this team that could have gone before us," Marchessault said. "It was a nice gesture, and I'm super happy it went that way. I couldn't be happier to do it with those six guys."

They'd grieved with the city in the wake of the October 1 massacre. They'd ridden the wave through a historic first season and endured the crushing defeat of losing in the Stanley Cup Final. They'd suffered playoff defeats of all shapes and sizes in 2019, 2020, and 2021. They missed the playoffs altogether in 2022.

Much had been said about the Golden Knights shipping players out of town left and right in their short existence. In reality, the organization's ability to keep those six players together demonstrates a rate of retention that few teams could match through the course of six NHL seasons.

"A lot of guys have gone through, right?" Carrier said after winning the championship. "Yeah, you're a survivor. You don't think about it. They try to have a winning team every year. They try to bring people in and pieces that can help us win. They believed in us right off the bat. We proved that we can win."

The journey from a pack of Misfits assembled from the NHL Expansion Draft to a star-studded championship group took

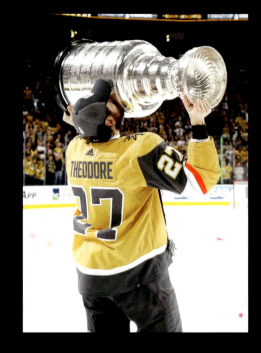

only six years. Half a dozen years isn't very long in the big picture of hockey history, but it's more than enough time to form unbreakable bonds. Teammates become friends. Friends become brothers. Brothers do whatever it takes to see each other succeed.

The Golden Misfits established the culture in Vegas that hasn't wavered in six years. It was only fitting that their hands were among the first to hold the Stanley Cup.

This is my occupation. This is what we do for a living. And how lucky are we to do this? That in the midst of trying to earn a living, you get to win a Stanley Cup. And being in the league is its own reward. Working in the NHL is its own reward. It's glorious. But when you win a Stanley Cup, there's just a whole new level and understanding of an experience that I don't know how to replicate in your life. And to be able to experience that once in your life, you are lucky indeed.

STONE I think everybody figured it was going to be the six Misfits that I handed the Cup to first. I don't think there was any debate there. You see guys pushing those guys – they didn't want to make a vote. And that's the kind of guys they are because

this is obviously a totally new team. But those guys have been creating the culture here from day one – creating and making this organization what it is, especially between the four walls in the locker room.

For me, personally, being on the leadership group with Reilly, him being a captain here since the opening night, I thought that he was the deserving guy to get the Cup next. That was my main reason – just the fact that he had been a part of that leadership group since the first game the Vegas Golden Knights ever played.

KARLSSON My speech after the parade, it came from the heart. I hadn't planned at all to speak on the stage, so it was just me speaking from my heart.

CAP-ROUGE TO CONN SMYTHE

Jonathan Marchessault became a draft-eligible player after the 2008-09 season when he had 53 points (18 goals, 35 assists) in 62 games for the Quebec Ramparts in the Quebec Major Junior Hockey League. **All 30 NHL teams passed on him.**

Surely a team would take him in his second year of draft eligibility after a 71-point season (30 goals, 41 assists) in 2009-10. But once again, players were selected – 210 of them – and none of them were named Marchessault.

In his final year of draft eligibility, Marchessault led the Ramparts in scoring with 95 points (40 goals, 55 assists) in 68 games, yet every NHL team passed on him for a third time.

In those three drafts, 641 players were selected. Only 39 of those players have more points than Marchessault in their respective NHL careers. Thirty-five players from those drafts are Stanley Cup Champions, and only Ryan O'Reilly and Victor Hedman have won the Conn Smythe Trophy.

When Marchessault skated over to commissioner Gary Bettman to receive the Conn Smythe as the most valuable player in the postseason, he became the first undrafted player to win the award since Wayne Gretzky achieved the feat in 1985 and 1988.

When Marchessault was awarded the Conn Smythe, he thanked Jack Eichel for helping him succeed in the playoffs. Eichel hugged him and told him, "It's the best thing I've ever seen."

Everyone knew, or could see, that I had a couple cups of confidence before going on that stage. I heard once that a drunk man's word is a sober man's thoughts.

It's been a long love story from day one between me and Vegas – all of us, really. I think that is exactly why it feels so good, because we were there from the start. We were there to help build it up from the beginning. To see how hockey has grown here in Vegas, there is so much that has happened. To top it off with the Stanley Cup is just magical. It means so much to me to win with Vegas, rather than any other organization, just because of that reason. It's not a lot of people who get to be there from the start with an organization and then to win as well.

MARCHESSAULT Honestly, all along in my career, I always had a chip on my shoulder. Every time, I was either not tall enough, not fast enough, or not good enough. I was never one of the best ones. I was always a decent player, but nothing like all the guys that were getting drafted. I was not expecting to get drafted – I wasn't even listed in the maybes.

They have guys listed in every round, every spot, and there's also maybes, and I wasn't even in those. I was not close to being in that situation.

I don't try to think too far ahead. I try to stay in the moment. The mentality that I have today is the same mentality I had all my life: What can I do to become better? That's always what's going to happen with me. Yeah, I've gone against a lot of odds.

Just to win the Stanley Cup, it's unbelievable. Any hockey player just wants to do that once in their life. It's so rare – we join an elite group of players, and it's something that's never going to go unnoticed. You work hard to get in that situation, and your name is engraved on the Cup. No one is going to take that away from you. That's probably the best part of it.

STONE If I'm getting offered a chance to take the Stanley Cup home, I'm taking it home. I was pretty excited. I didn't know that until Petro told me, "You get to sleep with that thing tonight." I was, like, "What?" He said, "Yeah." So I got to take it

OPPOSITE
Adin Hill enjoyed the parade before unveiling a vintage UNLV basketball jersey for the rally.

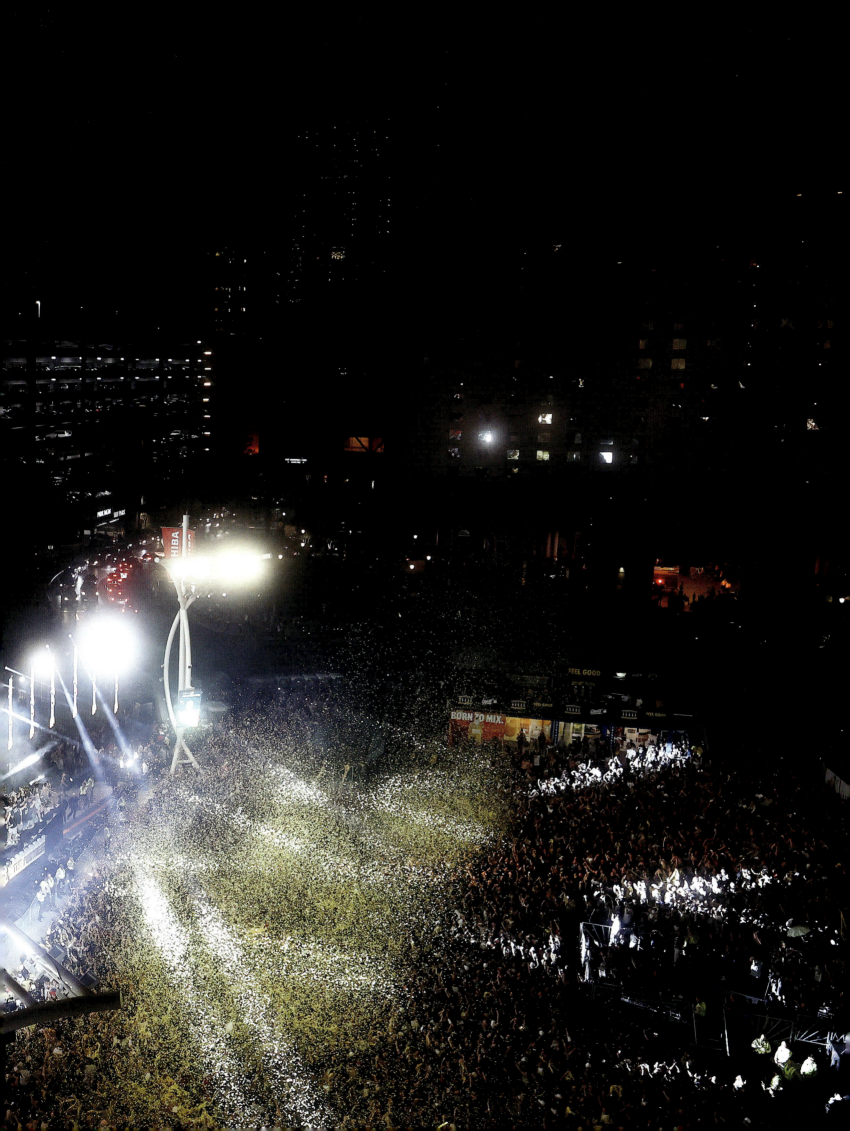

WILD BILL'S PROMISE

The Vegas Golden Knights and William Karlsson have had a symbiotic relationship since the organization selected him from the Columbus Blue Jackets in expansion.

Karlsson has produced on the ice for the Golden Knights and has been a staple in the locker room as a consistent face for six seasons. The city of Las Vegas has given back to Karlsson, as he met his wife, Emily, in 2017

and the couple brought baby Beckham into the world early in 2023.

Ahead of the 2019-20 season, he signed an eight-year contract to stay in Vegas. When he signed, Bill Foley smiled as he told him he expects three Stanley Cups in those eight years.

Karlsson helped the Golden Knights to the third round of the playoffs in 2020

and in 2021, but Vegas fell short of the goal on both occasions. After Karlsson missed the postseason in 2022, he and the Golden Knights hoisted the Stanley Cup as champions in 2023.

Foley and Karlsson greeted each other on the ice with smiles and hugs as they realized the goal they set out to achieve six seasons ago.

"That's one."

home and then got to talk to the keepers. That was a special night.

To be celebrating in the dressing room was just so different. You work, you grind, you're with those guys every single day for whatever it is – 250 days. Including training camp, probably closer to 300. You're with those guys every day. If you were to let me stay there, I'd still probably be sitting there with it right now with the guys and talking. Those are special moments – that's what you remember when you retire.

RYAN CRAIG When you win the Stanley Cup, it's the joy you get to see when you're sharing it with your family and friends. You just see how many people have supported you – the impact that it's had on you, you get to see that. And then it's the bond that's shared with championship teams, and it's a bond that will never be broken – however many years you're actually on the Cup, and then you're in the Hall of Fame together. I'll be beside John Stevens and Sean Burke. And it's a bond that you'll have. I mean, you can run into these people five years down the road and not have spoken to somebody, and that bond will pick up right where it is because of what we went through. I've been on teams that have gone to the Final and lost, and it won't be the same bond. It's getting over that final hill and that hump that really seals the bond.

JOHN STEVENS We come to the rink every day as coaches, and we're asking the players every day to try and get better. We're trying to be the best. And

we have a vision in mind. We do that every day – every day until we're done. And you finish the game and you're on top of the world. There's no better feeling in the world.

When you get to see it all come together and you win a championship, I think it bonds you forever – when you win the Stanley Cup, and you get the opportunity, share it, share the celebration, share the trophy, share everything with your family and friends that you care about. To me, it is the greatest pleasure – winning is the opportunity to share with so many.

EICHEL Winning trumps all. That feeling from the initial week after winning and those two months that we were playing in the playoffs, those were the two best months of my life. Thankfully, I got to experience it, because there are so many guys in the NHL who have fantastic careers, and so many friends of mine that have played for a while who haven't had the opportunity to do that.

I feel so grateful for having been part of the organization and team with so many great players. We had such a great team. I would give anything to be able to do that again multiple more times. That's what you want as a hockey player – you want to win.

For so many years of my career, everyone considered me a loser – not personally, but just a guy who didn't win. Suddenly, you win and the whole narrative changes. I was thinking about it last

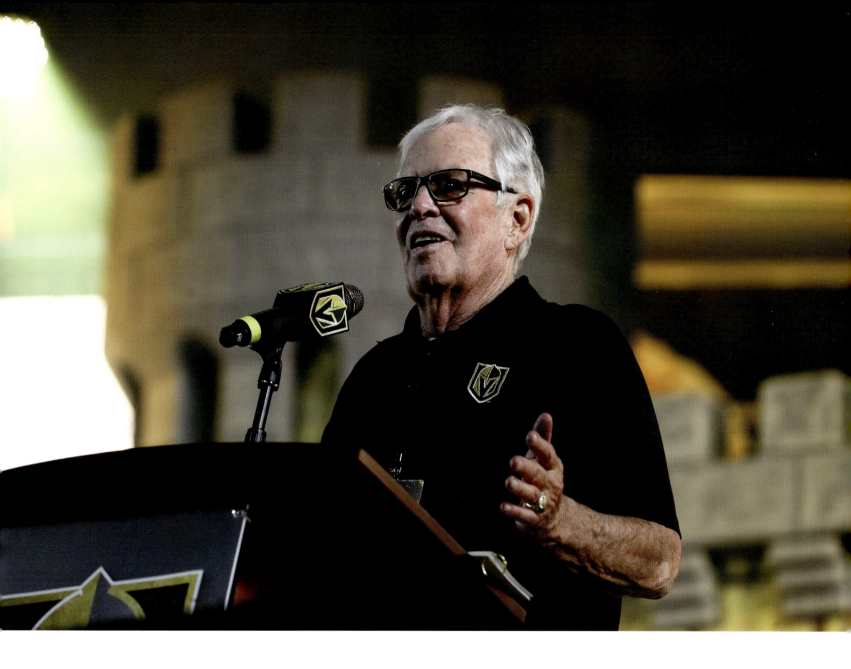

week, and after winning one, all I want to do now is do that again – have that feeling again, go through that experience again with the guys.

It's really hard to put into words. When you're going in the moment, you're just playing. Then, suddenly, you look, and you've won a series, two, three, and then you're in the Stanley Cup Final. Things change when you get to the Final – the feeling changes. Your emotions are different than they were during the first three rounds – that whole experience of going to the rink every day with the guys, knowing what you're playing for, knowing what's on the line. I think that trumps anything for me.

ALEC MARTINEZ On a personal level, I didn't know my wife when I won the first two in LA, but ever since we met and started dating, I've always said that I hoped that I was able to win one again just so she could experience it.

Not just the win, but the grind of the season and the ups and downs of the playoffs – obviously, the celebration too, and everything after.

When that clock is ticking down, celebrating on the ice and having your family out there, and all the festivities after, including the Cup parties, I always said that I wanted to do that. We were talking just the other day, and she said she had never really understood what I meant. Not that she just dismissed it, but she didn't understand, and she didn't know, because she had never gone through it before. Once we did win, and I was able to share that with her and she was able to see all that stuff, I think she finally understood, and she finally got it. That was really cool.

Obviously, I wasn't an original Misfit, but, being around for three years, Las Vegas truly is for me a special place to play. The way that the community

Bill Foley addressed the championship rally five days shy of seven years to the day after he was awarded an NHL franchise.

STONE WALL

Las Vegas was buzzing with excitement in the days after the Vegas Golden Knights won the Stanley Cup.

In the Arts District of Downtown Las Vegas, six artists collaborated on a mural to commemorate the championship their Golden Knights won for the city. The mural depicts a triumphant Mark Stone raising the Stanley Cup above his head, still clad in gold. Next to him is a play on the "Welcome to Fabulous Las Vegas" sign that instead reads "Home of the Champions: 2023 Stanley Cup."

Nine days after he received the Stanley Cup, Stone visited the mural, shook hands with the artists, and put the finishing touch on the piece: a spray-painted signature in gold in a spot they'd picked out for him.

rallies around the team, the support that we get from the fans – that was genuinely just really, really special to be a part of the first one for the Knights.

ADIN HILL In the moment, I'm not really thinking about what anyone else thinks – whether they think I am worthy of it or not. I'm just happy to be there, happy to share that with my teammates, my family. I mean, you grow up and from a young age, that's your dream about hockey, right? You obviously want to get drafted, make it to the NHL, play your first NHL game. Those are little things. But the main goal is to win the Stanley Cup.

It's pretty surreal. When you get that trophy in your hands, you get to lift it over your head. I mean, every year, once a year, you sit on your couch, and you watch the top team in the world do it. So to be able to experience that and have it be us raising it was awesome.

BEN HUTTON All the guys who weren't playing, we were looking for beers at the start of the third period. We were pretty jazzed up. We were, like, "Where are those beers? What is happening right now? Yeah, we did that."

But, honestly, we didn't really know what the heck we were doing. We were in the locker room, trying to figure out when to start getting dressed so we could be ready to go on the ice in our gear when the game ended for the celebration. We didn't exactly know what was going on, and the boys were still playing the game. We didn't really have anyone back there to tell us what was going on. We were just kind of running around like chickens with their heads cut off, just having a time in the back. And then, obviously, at the last minute or two, we joined the boys on the bench and then jumped on for the celebration. And that was incredible.

JACK EICHEL After the game, when everyone got back into the locker room and we were all in there together, that was pretty cool. There was even a short period where a lot of the media and cameras got kicked out. Mark Stone was putting the wig on, and that was a pretty sick moment. It was just the boys in there. We had just accomplished this, and he put the last puck up on the wall. Winning on the ice was pretty crazy. It's all such a blur, it happened so fast. Then he lifts up the Cup and says we're the greatest hockey team in the world. That says it all.

OPPOSITE
William Karlsson holds the Vegas records for goals in a season (43 in 2017–18) and best rally speech (in 2023).

ENGRAVED
FOREVER

BY BRUCE CASSIDY

I've been saying it for as long as I can remember: I want my name on the Stanley Cup. That's the goal - it always has been, and it always will be. It was all I could think about when first falling in love with the game, when my parents would drive me from rink to rink throughout Ottawa and beyond.

Now that my name is there and a childhood dream has become a reality, I'm able to realize what each name means and how those names truly represent so much more. When I look at my name on the Cup, I think about the number of people and amount of work it took to get me there.

Do you want to be a Stanley Cup champion, or not? That was my message to our team when we had a meeting at the hotel in Dallas the night before Game 6 of the Western Conference Final. I put some video clips together to show the guys first. They weren't pretty – we were losing the slot battle and getting pushed around in front of our net as part of a 4–2 loss on home ice. Then, we talked about legacies, a topic which seemed to grab the attention of the guys a lot more than the Game 5 highlights we had just played inside the hotel ballroom.

We talked about how hockey is never going to define you as a person. You're a husband, father, brother, son, but let's talk about our hockey family for now because that's why we're all here in Dallas. One day, you might be the guy that's on the outside looking in, wondering why your name never made it on the Cup. We're just one game away from going to the Stanley Cup Final. Let's think about what it means to us because now is the time to do something about it.

I knew it was a successful meeting that night because the guys were all paying attention and nodding their heads. You could tell they were thinking through the message and how it affected them personally. Every guy in that room was thinking about it a little bit different, but we left there with a common goal. We were ready to get it done the next night and advance to the Stanley Cup Final, and we did.

It was just the second time I had made it to hockey's biggest stage. The 2019 loss in Game 7 against St. Louis still hurts. It hurts to win, but it hurts to lose too. People ask me if winning with Vegas feels especially good after being let go by Boston, but the vindication for me was more about winning in the playoffs because that's where we fell short previously, like a lot of teams do. I only wanted to win to prove I could do it in April, May, and June.

We felt pretty good going into the Final against Florida. After our lone loss in Game 3, we handled it well. We gathered at the hotel the next day, and my message to them was simple: We didn't win that game. We should have, but we didn't. Let's play the same game again tomorrow, and the results will take care of themself. There was no panic in that room, and I think our guys weren't going to, regardless of what I said that day. We earned a gritty 3–2 win in a physical Game 4 to set us up for a night back in Vegas that we'll never forget.

My emotions aren't hard to figure out. When something bothers me, you can see it on the bench. Just ask our guys – I'm sure they'll agree with me on that one. When the final moments of Game 5 began to transpire on the bench, I started to think of those closest to me who made this all possible.

I looked up to where my family sits inside T-Mobile Arena. Julie, Shannon, and Cole have been there through thick and thin. They had to leave Boston, where our whole life was. Shannon and Cole were born in New England, and it was all they knew, from Providence to Boston. It can be tough on a parent when you see your kids making a change like that. You wonder, *Am I doing the right thing for them?* I was so happy for them because I knew how happy they were for me.

I started thinking about my parents that I lost a long time ago. They knew how much I loved hockey, and I wondered if they too were watching all of this happen. My dad passed when I was 21, but my mom saw me first get into coaching about 10 years later. She had seen so many ups and downs. She was still alive when I got fired in Washington and then passed while I was in Providence with the AHL affiliate of the Bruins.

I was just hoping that she was there with us to feel it and see it. I'm not an authority on the afterlife by any means, but I was hoping. *Hey, there, Mom! I made it!*

It hurts to win, although I can guarantee that we're going into next season with the intention of winning again. I want my name on the Stanley Cup again, and as you heard from my speech at the rally after the parade, I'm not going to hide from that. We're going to need a lot of things to go right, as they did this year, but that is our goal. When every guy steps on the ice and behind the bench next season, that's the goal. For me, it always has been, and it always will be.

THE NAMES
ON THE CUP

The recollections shared in the oral history portion of this book were gathered in the days and weeks following the Vegas Golden Knights winning the 2023 Stanley Cup championship in dozens of exclusive interviews with Gary Lawless. The essays by players and leadership (and Lil Jon) were contributed by each of those authors.

In some cases, quotations have been edited for space or clarity. To preserve their authenticity, some players' nicknames have been used in the quotes. While most of these are self-evident (*Stoney* for Mark Stone), we have included the nicknames used in parentheses in the list below for reference.

Bill Foley, Owner & Chairman
Robert Foley, Chief Business Officer
George McPhee, President of Hockey Operations
Kelly McCrimmon, General Manager
Bruce Cassidy, Head Coach (Butch)
John Stevens, Assistant Coach
Ryan Craig, Assistant Coach
Sean Burke, Director of Goaltending/NHL Goaltending Coach
Misha Donskov, Assistant Coach
Dave Rogowski, Video Coach
Kyle Moore, Associate Head Athletic Trainer
Mike Muir, Assistant Athletic Trainer
Raul Dorantes, Manual Therapist
Doug Davidson, Strength and Conditioning Coach
Aaron Heishman, Head of Sport Science and Reconditioning
Chris Davidson-Adams, Head Equipment Manager
J.W. Aiken, Assistant Equipment Manager
Rick Braunstein, Director of Team Services
Katy Headman Boettinger, Director of Hockey Administration
Vaughn Karpan, Assistant General Manager, Player Personnel
Bob Lowes, Assistant Director of Player Personnel
Scott Luce, Director of Amateur Scouting
Andrew Lugerner, Assistant General Manager
Wil Nichol, Director of Player Development
Tom Poraszka, Director of Hockey Operations

Mark Stone, Captain (Stoney)
Michael Amadio
Ivan Barbashev (Barbie)
Teddy Blueger
Laurent Brossoit (LB)
William Carrier
Paul Cotter
Jack Eichel (Eichs)
Nicolas Hague (Haguer)
Adin Hill (Hillsy, Hiller)
Brett Howden
Ben Hutton (Hutty)
William Karlsson (Karly)
Phil Kessel
Keegan Kolesar
Jonathan Marchessault (Marchy)
Alec Martinez (Marty)
Brayden McNabb (Nabber)
Brayden Pachal
Alex Pietrangelo (Petro)
Jonathan Quick (Quickie)
Nicolas Roy
Reilly Smith (Smitty)
Chandler Stephenson (Stevie)
Shea Theodore (Theo)
Logan Thompson (LT)
Zach Whitecloud (Whitey)

A CITY'S
CELEBRATION

BY MARK STONE

As I was riding in that convertible with Jack and Bill, headed toward the start of the parade, we knew we were in for something special. But we were kind of nervous, too, so we started joking with each other.

"I think we'll get 1,000, maybe 2,000, people out there," one of us said as we cruised down Frank Sinatra Drive.

"Maybe we can get lucky and 10,000 will come out," somebody else said with a laugh. We know this city, and we knew it would be a crowd.

Then we made that turn onto Flamingo Road, and you could already hear a bit of a roar. I started to think it might be even bigger than we expected. It was an energy, almost like the way the crowd was buzzing in the minute before Smitty's goal in Game 5.

Then that turn onto the Strip – I'll never forget that turn for the rest of my life. It could be years from now, taking my wife to dinner at the Bellagio or a show at the Cosmo, and I'll smile when I make that turn.

In a week full of memorable moments, you can't say it topped them all, when one of them was being handed the Stanley Cup. But leading a parade down the Las Vegas Strip with the Cup raised? Like I said, unforgettable.

The crowd was unreal. It always has been here. It's always been loud, it's always been sold out. But when I got here in 2019, I learned fast that it

ran deeper than that. You spend time around the community, and you see how much the Golden Knights mean to people here.

I hear about how other fans are frustrated that our fans only had to wait six years for this. But they clearly don't know Las Vegas and the people in Las Vegas. These fans – the people along Las Vegas Boulevard – they wanted it as badly as we did.

And that day, they wanted to celebrate as badly as we did.

Once we made that turn and started to take it all in – the fountains, the Eiffel Tower on the left, guys' pictures hoisting the Cup on every marquee – I started itching to get out of the car.

We wanted the fans to get to celebrate up close. I wanted to give some high-fives, share some drinks, spray some champagne. There are so many nights we feed off their energy at T-Mobile Arena. To be honest, with how hard we had partied that week, they were lifting us up again at the parade.

Bringing the Cup along the side of the road was important too. It's the hardest trophy to win in our sport, and just being around it is special. I know

that whole week, I wanted to go wherever it went. I wanted to share that feeling with as many people along that parade route as I could.

We also wanted the whole team to get the chance to celebrate with the Cup. We all had our family members and friends on those buses, and it was pretty cool to be able to enjoy the Cup in that setting with them.

So, pretty quickly, we had one more Cup handoff going, just like we did on the ice. I thought that was cool – a connection between each of us, from bus to bus, and from the team to the fans.

That day and night, the fans were the stars. We were the ones on the buses and onstage at the rally, yeah.

But it's the crowd, and the roar, and the overwhelming sense of joy as you looked at people that I'll remember. That's what people will talk about for years – well, that and Karly!

I mentioned that night onstage that no city throws a party like Vegas. I think that's what everybody wanted to see – how crazy will it be on the Strip?

It definitely exceeded expectations. And I can't wait to do it again.

VEGAS GOLDEN KNIGHTS

EDITORS:
Caylee Allard, Bailey Allen, Garrett Calloway, Nate Ewell, Brady Hackmeister, Zak Krill, Gary Lawless, Ryan Levine, Songee Pak, Stephanie Rogers, India Shay, Eric Tosi, Gordon Weigers

WRITERS/CONTRIBUTORS:
Kerry Bubolz, Garrett Calloway, Bruce Cassidy, Paul Cotter, Jack Eichel, Nate Ewell, Bill Foley, Lil Jon, Gary Lawless, Jonathan Marchessault, Kelly McCrimmon, George McPhee, Mark Stone, Gordon Weigers

VEGAS GOLDEN KNIGHTS wish to thank Bill Foley and the Foley family, Jeff Bottari, Kerry Bubolz, Kris Knief, Zak Krill, Chip Seigel, Maggie Sweeney, all the players, staff and celebrities who contributed to this book, the entire Foley Entertainment Group team, the National Hockey League, NHL Images, and Getty Images

Skybox Press wishes to acknowledge Vince & Diana Nalbone, Lizter Van Orman, and Chris Orlando

PHOTOGRAPHY

Vegas Golden Knights: Jeff Bottari, David Becker, And Zak Krill; **National Hockey League via Getty Images:** David Becker, Jeff Bottari, Sam Hodde, Dave Sandford, Eliot J. Schechter; **Getty Images Sport:** Joel Auerbach, Bruce Bennett, Joshua Bessex, Ethan Miller, Christian Petersen, Candice Ward; **Associated Press:** Abbie Parr

SKYBOX PRESS

Editor & Publisher: Scott Gummer
Design: Nate Beale/SeeSullivan
Project Manager: Rachel Lopez Metzger
Copyeditor: Mark Nichol

www.skyboxpress.com
info@skyboxpress.com
(707) 537-8700

ISBN: 979-8-9850412-9-3

Printed in the United States of America

10 9 8 7 6 5 4 3 2

Published by Skybox Press, LLC.